Soul**Work**

Deborah P. Bloch

Soul**Work**

Finding the Work You Love, Loving the Work You Have

Deborah P. Bloch

Lee J. Richmond

Davies-Black Publishing
Palo Alto, California

Published by Davies-Black Publishing, an imprint of Consulting Psychologists Press, Inc., 3803 East Bayshore Road, Palo Alto, CA 94303; 800-624-1765.

Special discounts on bulk quantities of Davies-Black books are available to corporations, professional associations, and other organizations. For details, contact the Director of Book Sales at Davies-Black Publishing, an imprint of Consulting Psychologists Press, Inc., 3803 East Bayshore Road, Palo Alto, CA 94303; 650-691-9123; fax 650-988-0673.

02 01 00 99 98   10 9 8 7 6 5 4 3 2 1
Printed in the United States of America

Library of Congress Cataloging-in-Publication Data
Bloch, Deborah P.
      Soul Work : finding the work you love, loving the work you have /
Deborah P. Bloch, Lee J. Richmond.
            p.   cm.
      Includes bibliographical references.
      ISBN 0-89106-119-3 (pbk.)
      1. Career changes. 2. Vocational guidance. 3. Spiritual life.
      I. Bloch, Deborah Perlmutter. II. Richmond, Lee Joyce.
HF5384.S65   1998
650.14—dc21
                                                                                    98-18576
                                                                                    CIP

FIRST EDITION
First printing 1998

Contents

Read Me: The Keys to Understanding
the Rest of the Book   vii

Acknowledgments   xi

About the Authors   xiii

1   **Change:** Allison's Awakening   1

2   **Balance:** Helen on the High Wire   33

3   **Energy:** Bob's Barbeque   61

4   **Community:** Beatrice at the Beginning   85

5   **Calling:** Manny the Millionaire   111

6   **Harmony:** David in the Dollhouse   141

7   **Unity:** Kevin Crashes   175

Bibliography   205

Read Me

The Keys to Understanding
the Rest of the Book

■ Information surrounds us. But where is knowledge? With technology we can produce more and more. But what is its worth? The means of communication increase. But what are we saying? The questions of knowledge, worth, and content are questions of meaning.

■ Questions of meaning are spiritual questions. Spirituality is the experience of connection to something that transcends our ordinary lives. We may envision this connection to something larger than ourselves or deeper within ourselves, but we know it is beyond the material.

■ Because of the centrality of work in our lives, the questions of meaning or the quest for the spiritual are more valuable than questions of ability and interest in our search for knowledge, worth, and content in our careers. Indeed, questions of ability and interest are part of the spiritual quest.

■ This is the same spiritual quest whose story has been told countless times. It is the story of the quest for the Holy Grail, for the lost temple, for the truth hidden behind a door. So this book connects the search for meaning in work to the universal spiritual quest. That quest is to understand who we are in relationship to all that is. What is each person's place in the continuing creation of the cosmos? How can each person's work be connected to the unfolding story of humankind? That is what this book is about.

■ At the same time, this is a personal book for each reader. It will draw you from the universal questions of connections between spirit and career to the dilemmas you face in your work and from these dilemmas to practical solutions. It will help you see that you are not alone in your search for meaning in work and spirituality in your career.

■ This book presents the connections between spirit and work organized into the seven themes of the seven chapters. Seven emerged as the right number of chapters because it resonates spiritually in many traditions. There is a completeness and unity in the seven days of the week. The Catholic religion celebrates seven sacraments. The seven-branched candelabra is the symbol of Judaism. The Book of Revelation depends heavily on the repetition of the pattern of sevens. There are seven wise men of ancient Greece and seven wonders of the world. The particular themes of the seven chapters came from our knowledge of career development, of spiritual traditions, and our intuitive sense of what was right for this book as it emerged in the writing process.

How to Read This Book

The following are some unique characteristics of this book. Understanding them will help you get the most out of it.

■ The book is written to you, the reader. So when the authors say "you," they really mean you, and not some general other person. When the authors say "we," they mean themselves, or you and themselves.

- The book is not only about work in general or a particular job you may hold or be seeking. It is about the totality of career and its place in your life.

- Career does not fall into neat stages where first we are students, then workers, then retirees. Our experience tells us that people move back and forth between stages and are often in more than one stage at a time. We prefer to think of a career as a path that embraces seven spiritual and pragmatic themes: change, balance, energy, community, harmony, calling, and unity. These are the seven themes of this book, and each theme is explored in a chapter. Feel free to start with the theme that most immediately meets your needs, and read the chapters in the order you like.

- Each chapter is made up of four sections. First there is a story about a person who faces a career dilemma and receives guidance from an unexpected source, a wise person. Look for the wise person who gives guidance in each story. Then there are brief lists of the career issues faced by the person in the story and related issues faced by people in general. We recommend reading the story before you look at the career issues. But if that is not your style, use the book in the way you prefer. The next section of each chapter is a set of reflections that draw on career theory, poetry, philosophy, psychology, physics, music, and everything else we know to explain the connections among career, meaning, spirituality, and the particular theme of the chapter. The last part of each chapter is made up of applications, exercises that challenge your thinking and your feeling. All the career issues presented early in each chapter are reflected in that chapter's applications.

- Just as there is no one straight career path, there is no single road to career success and meaning for everyone. Do not expect to find a universally applicable list of do's and don'ts in this book. Any list that applies to everyone also applies to no one. You will find that each chapter contains applications. Complete the applications and you will find your own path.

▌ A special feature of the applications is a meditation on the theme of each chapter. The focus of the meditation is on opening one of the seven energy centers in your body. These energy centers, or *chakras*, have been used as a focus of meditation for centuries in both Buddhist and Hindu traditions. Similar visualizations have been used within the mystical literature of the Judeo-Christian tradition. Using each particular energy center as a metaphor, you reach the essence of the chapter theme in a nonintellectual way. At the same time, you bring balance to your body and your mind. In the meditations in this book, each energy center is pictured as located in a part of the body and is associated with a color and particular aspects of spiritual, emotional, and physical health as understood through the practice of the authors.

When to Read This Book

Read this book when you are on your journey of career change. You may embark on this journey because of external pressures or because you just feel ready for some difference in your life. You can choose to go on the journey blindfolded, stumbling on rocks, sloshing through muddy puddles, or you can go open-eyed, with the maps of the book to guide you. Although each person makes the journey alone, you can take this book as a companion to alleviate the loneliness of the road.

Acknowledgments

Writing any book draws on the experience and knowlege the authors have accumulated over their lifetimes. Writing this book led us into the wellspring of our own spiritual growth.

Deborah Bloch: I thank my grandfather, Isaac Ricklin, who taught me, by example, the meaning of having a good soul. I thank my mother, Lillian Weinstock, for, among so many other things, introducing me to the riches found in books. I thank all who are in my life—my husband, Martin Bloch; my sons, Michael and Kenneth Perlmutter; Kenneth's wife, Jacqueline; my grandsons, David and Jeffrey; my friends; my colleagues; and my students—for their warmth, their ideas, and their laughter. I offer a particular note of appreciation to Joyce Pinkney, a Graduate Merit Scholar at the University of San Francisco, who helped with many of the details of proofreading and reference checking.

Lee Richmond: I acknowledge and thank my parents, Anne and Alexander Blank, who along with friends Mary Ellen Stephenson, Lenore Lynch, and Sister Margie Downs have loved and taught me in the past. I acknowledge also the students, colleagues, and friends who play and learn with me in the present. They know who they are. And I acknowledge my children,

Ruth Wexler, Stephen Richmond, Sharon Blaustein, and Jessica Mullaney, who, along with their spouses, Barry, Lynne, Eddie, and Martin, and their children, Bryan, Andrea, Alanna, Samantha, Allyson, Ryan, Rachel, and Robert, bring me daily joy and a spiritual hope for the future.

We both thank Melinda Adams Merino, Acquisitions Editor at Davies-Black, who recognized the importance of spirituality and career, and developed, encouraged, and supported our work.

About the Authors

Deborah P. Bloch, Ph.D., has focused her work on the career development of individuals and the organizational structures that promote a healthy work environment. Four of her books designed to help people find the jobs that are right for them have sold more than 150,000 copies.

Dr. Bloch is associate professor of organization and leadership at the University of San Francisco. Previously, she taught at Baruch College of the City University of New York. In addition to her university work, Dr. Bloch has worked as a consultant in the United States and abroad. She has served as president of both the National Career Development Association (NCDA) and the Association of Computer-Based Systems for Career Information, and she is a member of the editorial board of the *Career Planning and Adult Development Journal.* Dr. Bloch has received the Distinguished Service Award of the Association of Computer-Based Systems for Career Information, the Resource Award of the Career Planning and Adult Development Network, and the Merit Award of the NCDA.

Her work includes many published professional articles and numerous workshops for counselors and others who help people with their career decisions and job searches.

Other books by Dr. Bloch include the following, all published by NTC/Contemporary Publishing:

- *How to Write a Winning Resume* (now in its fourth edition)

- *How to Have a Winning Job Interview* (now in its third edition)

- *How to Make the Right Career Moves* (suggestions for people in midcareer)

- *How to Get a Good Job and Keep It* (help for high school students and others just starting out)

Lee J. Richmond, Ph.D., is a National Certified Career Counselor, a Certified Professional Counselor, and a Licensed Psychologist. She is professor of education at Loyola College in Baltimore, Maryland; she also conducts a private practice. Dr. Richmond has served as a consultant and trainer in career development, career assessment, and management training for several large corporations.

Past president of both the American Counseling Association (ACA) and the National Career Development Association (NCDA), Dr. Richmond currently chairs the Professional Standards Committee of NCDA. She also chairs the ACA Insurance Trust and is chair-elect of the board of the Career Development Training Institute.

Dr. Richmond has coedited three books and has authored many book chapters and articles, and she has more than thirty years of experience in the field.

The combined work experience of the authors includes not only more than sixty years in the field counseling, consulting, and teaching from the high school level through the postgraduate level but jobs as a department store salesperson, telephone switchboard operator, bookkeeper, temporary office worker, market research field worker and field supervisor, and administrator of women's programs, computer-based career information programs, research programs in career education, and university and college programs and divisions. Together they edited *Connections Between Spirit and Work in Career Development* (Davies-Black Publishing, 1997).

Change

Allison's Awakening

The Story

Allison wiped the last bits of shaving cream from Steven's ears with the soft white cloth he seemed to like best. She kissed the top of his head as she wheeled him from the bathroom to the front hall. He twisted his head up at her and smiled, or so she hoped. It might have been another of the spasms that twisted his face and body throughout the day and even in his sleep.

Allison wondered if Steven understood that this day would change his routine—and hers—forever. Steven, at nineteen, could speak only with difficulty, and it seemed that Allison was the only one who understood him. He could not walk or feed himself, and all the daily business of Steven's life had fallen to Allison. Of course, she thought, I wanted those so-called burdens. They brought the joy of knowing he had the best life he could with the disabled body and mind he was born with. She knew which foods he seemed to like and how to mash them so he could still taste the separate bananas and strawberries, yet swallow them without choking. She knew that he liked the blue

1

soft pants best and had bought them for him in larger and larger sizes as he grew from childhood to boyhood and now to manhood.

Now she realized that as Steven grew larger, she no longer grew stronger. She remembered how, through the years, she had marveled at the increasing strength in her arms, her back, her legs. They seemed to strengthen exactly as she needed them to, bearing more weight as Steven grew. She sometimes felt that the physical bond during pregnancy, the umbilical cord between her body and Steven's, had never been severed. Now Allison thought, I have grown older. Strength did not keep increasing. Her back had given out twice—that she admitted. Steven would have to be placed in a "full-care facility." The very term shook her. It seemed so hard, so impersonal. She tried to think of it as a "home" but that brought up other images she didn't like.

Allison's thoughts were interrupted by the bell. A glance out the window showed her the brown van and the lettering "Rosedale Farms." As she opened the door, Steven looked up at her with a question in his eyes, she thought.

He said, "Mmm."

And she answered, "Yes, Mommy's here and will always be here. But, remember, I told you that today we are going to a new home, where you will get everything you need, and there will be other people for you to be with. And there will be strong nurses to lift you in and out of bed, and give you baths. I've put everything you like in this suitcase."

Shirley, the social worker who had finally convinced Allison that she could no longer care for Steven at home, was at the door, along with a fit-looking young man she introduced as Jack. Allison began to push Steven's chair out of the house, but Jack gently shouldered her aside and wheeled him away. As they rode to Rosedale Farms, Shirley and Allison reviewed all that Rosedale Farms would do for Steven.

Leaving Steven at Rosedale was the most difficult thing Allison had ever done. She felt split in two. She barely remembered how she got home that first time. But the bus ride became familiar to her as the weeks passed and she regularly visited Steven. To her surprise, he seemed just the same as he had been at home.

It was really Allison's life that changed. There were many empty hours and days, time in which she had cared for Steven. She had no other routines, little to do. She was used to making do with little beyond the life insurance income her husband had left her. Now she wondered if that would be sufficient. What if Steven needed additional care? What would happen when she died? She began to look at ads in the newspaper. The years of caring for Steven did not seem to have prepared her for "wrd prfct windows, $16/hr" or "Retail/Sales: Your talents deserve the best." What did all of that mean? Just about nothing to Allison.

She thought she'd like to do what Shirley did. She liked how Shirley listened to her whole story, over many visits, without interrupting her or rushing her. She admired Shirley's knowledge of how Steven could be helped. For days she thought about Shirley. She sometimes saw her at Rosedale, but Shirley was always busy helping patients or their families. And when Allison spoke to Shirley, she felt it would be cheating to talk about herself rather than Steven.

However, one day, when Shirley asked Allison, "How are *you* doing?" all of Allison's thoughts came tumbling out. Allison ended, "I wish I could be like you, able to help people, be patient with them, and really know what I am doing."

"Why not?" Shirley asked. "You certainly are patient. Look at how you cared for Steven, the time it took, all you taught him. That took incredible reserves of patience."

"Okay, I'll grant that I'm patient, but that doesn't give me the knowledge to say the right things."

"I learned all of that during my six years of study to become a social worker. It took four years of college and then two years of graduate study to do it. If you want to become a social worker, you'll have to use your patience for yourself. Think first about going to community college. You can start by looking at the bulletin of Sussex Community College. Isn't that the one near you? It may help you with your thinking about what you want to do."

Allison left Rosedale no closer to an idea of what she could do. How could she possibly consider six years of school when she was already forty-four?

The next morning, in her new routine of morning coffee and paper, she saw an ad that seemed sent to her. The ad said: "Women's Programs: Thinking of returning to school? Think Sussex Community College. Call 555-2387."

The college catalog arrived a few days later. Allison looked through it and then looked in the mirror. What was the use? A few days later, Allison prepared for her bus ride to Rosedale. She grabbed the catalog as something to read on the way.

Allison boarded the bus and looked for an empty seat. Only one. It was next to one of those young men, really boys, she instinctively distrusted. His hair was orange. His tee shirt was tattered. His jeans hung loose around him, and a giant key chain dangled from his waist. His high-top sneaker laces lay open. She looked around again. No place else to sit. Without looking at her seat mate, she sat down and opened the catalog. She wanted to separate herself from the boy sitting next to her.

"Yo, lady," he said. "You thinking of sending your kid to that school? I go there."

It was too much. Her boy was in a full-care facility. This jerk went to college. Something made her say. "No, young man, I was actually looking at this for myself."

"Cool, man. What are you going to like study?"

"Nothing!" Allison said. She was overcome with bitterness.

He looked at her. "What do you mean? Are you coming to school and studying 'nothing'? That makes no sense."

"Look, it's none of your business. But what I mean is I'm not coming to school. There's no use in my studying what I want to study. I'd be fifty when I finished."

"Well, look, I know this isn't my business, just like you said, but the way I figure it you'll be fifty either way, if you're lucky, when you finish or when you don't finish."

Career Issues

In the story, Allison faced two major questions:

▪ How was she going to move from a life centered on the care of her son to a life in which she found fulfillment from paid work?

▪ Was she too old to go back to school and make the kind of change that would bring her satisfaction and success in work?

Here are some related career issues that many people face:

▪ Assuming new roles in life

▪ Letting go of old definitions of self

▪ Letting go of outworn images that limit the future

▪ Letting go of past work roles that are no longer productive

▪ Staying current and accepting the place of education and training in our work lives

▪ Understanding the importance of work and why we do it

Reflections

This story illustrates one of the central themes of this book: change. On the one hand, we want to hold on to our essential core, that which makes each one of us a "me." On the other hand, we recognize that sometimes we want to change. We may want to change in order to come closer to our individual ideal selves, or to meet new external situations and surroundings.

To change, we may have to let go of some part of ourselves or of something or someone we hold dear. We often feel that the parts we must relinquish are like the roots of a tree. We fear that if we give them up, or change them, like an uprooted tree we will perish. But just as the roots of many trees reach far beneath

To change, we often have to let go of some part of ourselves or of something or someone we hold dear.

the earth and thus are not seen, so too do our roots reach deep. They reach deep into our history, deep into the strengths we have developed throughout our lives, deep into our spirituality, and deep into all that nourishes each of us. We can call all of this the abundance of the universe. We cannot see the depth of the roots, but if, despite our fear, we act on faith that the universe will provide for us, we find that this is true. Our roots are deeper than we thought they were.

How can we experience the depth of our unseen roots? We can do so by becoming aware of our own stories and what they tell us about ourselves. We can also get in touch with our strengths through meditation. In the introduction to this book, we presented the idea of energy centers, or chakras. Each energy center is located in a particular part of the body and is associated with a color and aspects of one's physical, mental, and spiritual life. The first energy center is at the base of the spine, in many ways the root of the body. Opening this energy center puts us in touch with all the material abundance of the world in which we live. Material abundance includes not only money and what money can buy, but the very earth itself, the air we breathe, and all that is tangible, from fishes in the ocean to the book you are holding. Later, in the meditation at the end of this chapter, you will see how to use the first energy center to connect yourself to the material abundance of the world.

As we look at change in our own lives, we can examine how our image of ourselves contributes to our willingness to change, how our emotional roots affect change, how changes related to work affect us, and how the universe prepares the way for our change through synchronicity. In this set of reflections, these are the major concepts you will find:

▪ Change and Self-Image

▪ Change and Emotional Roots

▪ Change and Work

▪ Change and Synchronicity

Change and Self-Image

Allison was Sleeping Beauty. While she may or may not have been a physical beauty, something beautiful lay dormant in her the many years she was caring for Steven. The boy on the bus, in his oversized jeans and Dennis Rodman hair, gave her the prince's kiss of awakening. She would be fifty under any circumstances. What did she want to do with the rest of her years?

The tale of Allison, like the tale of Sleeping Beauty, helps us see two ideas: that anyone can be awakened by the kiss or call of the prince, and that the prince himself wears many different faces. Indeed, in other fairy tales, it is the prince, imprisoned in the body of the frog, who is awakened by the kiss of the princess. Another version of the same story is "Beauty and the Beast." The prince imprisoned in the body of a beast is freed by the love of a beautiful girl. The second idea is that it is never too late in life to change. It is never too late to pursue the work that speaks to us from inside ourselves. Let's look at that idea the other way

around as well. We are called to recognize our strengths, and it
is never too late to hear that call.

We all know the story of Ulysses, who left home to fight in
the Trojan War and had to face sirens, a one-eyed monster, and
other terrors before he could make his journey home. It is the
story of a virile, powerful young man and his companions. But

*It is never too late in life to change. It is never too late to
pursue the work that speaks to us from inside ourselves.*

what happens after Ulysses returns home? Do he and his patient
wife, Penelope, slip gracefully into old age, sitting before the fires
of their castle? Centuries after Homer told his tale, Tennyson
(1951/1832) wrote a poem in the voice of the older Ulysses, still
restless, still seeking work. He says, "I cannot rest from travel: I
will drink/life to the lees." He leaves his kingdom to his son, goes
down to the port, and prepares to set sail once again. He says to
his seamen, "you and I are old:/Old age hath yet his honour and
his toil:/Death closes all: But something ere the end,/Some work
of noble note, may yet have to be done,/Not unbecoming men
that strove with Gods."

As the young man said on the bus, "You're going to be fifty,
if you're lucky, whether you finish or not." Allison in her mind
was able to add the unsaid, "Why not do some work 'of noble
note'?" Ulysses was a mortal, like Allison, like you and me. We
can make the assumption that for most people, physical strength
begins to diminish somewhat in late middle age. This decrease
in physical prowess is not associated with a loss of intelligence,
creativity, or the ability to understand and appreciate the sacred-
ness of life. On the contrary, contributions "of noble note" are
made throughout the life span. Consider Grandma Moses, who
began painting in her seventies. Not only was she a farm wife,
untrained in art, but her pictures are those of a young person,
full of the simplicity, energy, and life of the rural world she
knew. Her style has influenced many artists, and her work is
acclaimed worldwide. Pablo Casals, who began his concert career

as a cellist, continued to conduct orchestras through his eighties. George Burns, who played God Himself, provided entertainment through movies, television, and personal appearances well into his nineties. In other words, people of all ages can choose to do meaningful work. Indeed, as Tennyson suggested, we need to continue to do meaningful work at all ages in order to feel complete.

It is sometimes difficult for us to value ourselves at all ages. We all know that the media favors the young. But each of us chooses how we respond to those media messages. Surely we do not drink every brand of beer, buy every car, or eat every snack advertised. We do not live our lives to match the afternoon "soaps" or the evening comedies on television. Similarly, we do not have to buy into the culture of youth. We have the capacity to value the beauty in ourselves at every age. Do we actually know what age Sleeping Beauty was when the prince kissed her? Can you visualize your prince or princess kissing you now? What is the beauty sleeping within you?

Age is not the only personal factor that may affect our self-image. Any time we think we are less because we do not fit some external model, we are limiting our opportunities unnecessarily.

Popular music has not only glorified youth, but also the later part of life. Listen to the words of "September Song." It's a familiar beginning: "Oh it's a long long time from May to December, and the days dwindle down when they reach September." Then throughout the song, those September days are called "those precious days," "those precious few." Allison realizes finally the preciousness of her days, and the fact that they are fewer makes them more precious, not less.

Age is not the only personal factor that may affect our self-image. Any time we think we are less because we do not fit some external model, we are limiting our opportunities unnecessarily. Do you think you are too fat, too tall, too short? Is your hair too limp, too curly, too sparse? As soon as we think *too*, as in *too much* or *too little*, we are comparing ourselves to artificial, mental standards we have chosen to accept from our particular culture. You may be thinking that others do have those standards and that is just the way the world operates. You may think it is impossible to overcome the cultural stereotypes. Well, consider actor Peter Falk and listen to his pronunciation of the letter *l*. He has turned what most would consider a speech impediment into a signature style of speaking. Look at actors Roseanne and Danny DeVito. If you had been their high school teacher, would you have recommended they choose acting as a career? Ask yourself how you may be limiting your opportunities for change because you are accepting a limitation based on an artificial standard.

Change and Emotional Roots

When we are awakened to change within ourselves, we recognize that others around us will both affect the change and be affected by it. In changing ourselves, we may have to modify or relinquish emotional ties that we thought were unbreakable. Relinquishing a tie to someone is not the same as giving up or giving up on the person. What we mean is that the nature of the emotional content of the relationship may change. As we go through the process of change, we may discover that roots we thought were unbreakable are really nearer the surface and can be dug up without too much pain. But we also may discover the

When we are awakened to change within ourselves, we recognize that others around us will both affect the change and be affected by it.

strength of other roots, roots that continue to nourish us. Sometimes we don't know the difference between the surface roots and the deeper roots until change is forced on us.

People facing divorce or the breakup of a long-term couple relationship often fear that they will simply not survive the severing of the bonds to the other person. They imagine themselves as drifting through life in a torrent of tears. They cannot picture going on without the support of the person they counted on. But then, as they are forced to stand on their own, they discover that they were never as supported as they thought they had been. The support had come from within themselves. On the other hand, even after the death of a partner who truly was supportive, the survivor sometimes recognizes how he or she has incorporated the partner's support. It becomes a part of the survivor's own being, the survivor's rootedness. When we recognize strength in others, we can incorporate that strength into ourselves. It is what we do when we admire heroes and heroines in books or movies.

In our story, Allison found rootedness in herself when she gave up her old notions of duty to her son. Letting go of children is perhaps the second most difficult task in life. The first most difficult task is letting go of our dependence on our parents when we were children. We did not suddenly walk out the door, get jobs, and find homes of our own. First we learned to walk without leaning on Mommy or Daddy. We learned how to play with

When we recognize strength in others, we can incorporate that strength into ourselves. It is what we do when we admire heroes and heroines in books or movies.

other children and we went to school. Of course, the first time we clung tightly to the hand of an adult. But it is unlikely that you went to high school holding on to your parent's hand. By the time you got to high school, you had learned how to complete complex tasks all on your own. Throughout this period of growth, you were gaining a sense of who you are. Finally, you were ready to step out on your own. Erik Erikson (1963) has described these developmental tasks in terms of stages through which we pass during our life span. However, another set of developmental tasks and stages faces us as we raise our own children. To be supportive of children and teenagers means letting go in stages. While there are many books on how to raise children, few deal with the issues of supporting and letting go at the same time. Allison's experience may have been extreme because of the unusual level of Steven's need. But the importance of her letting go so that both of them could move to more productive lives is no different from that of any parent.

Change and Work

We have been discussing holding on to our emotional roots as we let go of outmoded family roles. The same principles that we explored in discussing family and couple situations apply to job change. The impetus for changing jobs may be internal as you seek growth or difference in what you do. Although you have chosen to make the change, you may still experience anxiety or discomfort. You may be unsure of how the change you are seeking will affect your life or your sense of yourself. While you may feel prepared for the new tasks, you may still experience feelings of doubt about your performance once you are on the job. You may be unclear about the direction you want to take or the steps you need to take to reach a goal. Your feelings about the change may be more overwhelming than the actual change itself will be.

On the other hand, the impetus for change may be an external event forcing the change on you. You may find yourself without a job because the company you work for is going out of business, moving to another part of the country, or changing the size or nature of its workforce. You may also lose your job because the person you work for does not appreciate your contributions. Everyone finds this unsettling at best. Many people experience emotions similar to the grieving after the death of a loved one. These emotions include anger, resentment, and sadness, sometimes even despair. What can you do?

In either case, the first thing to do is to acknowledge what you are feeling. As soon as you begin to do this, you are putting yourself in touch with your emotional roots. Some people need to express what they are feeling to someone they trust. Others prefer to keep the feelings inside and sort them out themselves. There is no right or wrong way to deal with the feelings as long as you become aware of what they are. You will know you are ready to move to the next step when you stop concentrating only on your emotions and begin to think about what you can do next.

After dealing with your emotions, you may find that being fired brings an opportunity for change for the better. In one instance, a major steel company was cutting back on the number of people it employed. Because there were so many unemployed people in the town, the community college decided to provide a meeting for all those who needed help. Over two thousand people showed up. The main speaker at the conference talked about losing your job as the opportunity to do something you have always wanted to do. Many people came to talk to the speaker after her formal talk. One person stood out as particularly animated. A man in his late thirties said he had always been interested in cars, particularly T-birds, and he was now going to try to get a job with a dealership. Six months later the speaker got a letter from the man thanking her and offering her a "deal" the next time she wanted a Ford car.

The steelworker–turned–car salesman heard something in the speaker's words that spoke directly to him just as Allison heard a special message from the young man on the bus. To both the man at the conference and Allison the message was a call for change that seemingly came from the universe.

There are other considerations besides emotions that are important in bringing about successful change in work. Whether you are choosing to change or the choice has been made for you, being up to date is essential. In our story, Allison is stymied when she first considers what kind of job she would like. She cannot read the jargon of the want ads. And she knows that she is completely unfamiliar with computers. In today's job market, there is almost no field of work or any level of job that does not require some computer ability. You may not even recognize that the tool you are using is a computer. Salespeople now operate specially designed computers that record the sale, provide receipts, process charges, and control inventory. They have taken the place of cash registers. Automobile repair people need to be familiar with the electronic systems that run today's cars.

There are many ways to keep current. One way is to study on your own. If you plan to stay in your own field, there may be books or other publications that will provide the information you need. In addition, many companies provide workshops for their employees. Take advantage of any training that is offered by your

Part of staying current is knowing what is required of you for the occupational goal you have set.

organization. Community colleges offer occupational training that ranges from a single course over several weeks to degree programs that require the equivalent of two years of full-time study. Like Allison in our story, you may want to make a switch to an occupation that requires particular study at the undergraduate or graduate level. The occupation may require licensing or certification. Part of staying current is knowing what is required of you for the occupational goal you have set.

People can learn what is required of them from newspapers, magazines, and discussions with others. However, there is a whole world of career information. We provide help for you in getting to career information in Chapter 6, "Harmony."

When Allison got her information and decided to make a change in her occupation, she was also making a decision to change other parts of her routine. Women who have worked only in their homes for many years face particular changes. Instead of working to their own schedules and family-established routines, they must now respond to the time demands of the outside world. Responsibilities for housekeeping and cooking do not usually disappear but must be worked into an already tiring day or week. While this is a common change for women, men may also experience major disruptions of routine as a result of work changes. Changes in shift, for example, often cause disruptions in sleeping and other physical functions. Our bodies accustom themselves to whatever schedule we follow. When we change shifts, it can be likened to a major case of jet lag. Change in job location requiring either more or less travel can also affect your routines and family interactions. People who move from highly structured organizations like the military into less formally organized work situations have to learn new ways of relating to their co-workers, their bosses, and the workers who report to them. People who have worked in offices and who are now working from home have to find new ways to maintain a structure in their time. They often have to rearrange their homes to accommodate the tasks of work. And family relationships can be strained when a family member is at home but not available because he or she is working.

Two big questions remain: What is work? and Why work at all? Work is the production of something or the accomplishment of some goal through physical or mental effort. Notice that work can be paid or unpaid. It can be carried out for someone else or on your own behalf. It can involve the tangible, the production of something, or the intangible, the accomplishment of a goal. Work can mean putting forth an idea. Plato worked. When human beings work, they put forth effort. If effort is not needed, then why work at all? The answer is simple: Human beings work because they see there is work to be done. Indeed it is the nature of all living beings to work. That is the spirituality of work. It is through work that living beings express who and what they are all about. And it is through work that living beings participate in the ongoing co-creation of the universe. Of course, most people find it necessary to work for pay. When Allison gets a paying job, she will be able to have more material goods than she had before.

Human beings work because they see there is work to be done.

She is concerned about providing future care for her son. But that is not the primary reason why she is considering becoming a social worker, a goal that will be difficult to achieve. Her goal of becoming of a social worker is wrapped up in her sense of what she can do and what needs doing.

As you think back over your own life, you can probably identify the times that you have worked because you felt something needed doing and you knew you could do it. It was in you to do. As you read the chapters in this book, you will find more and more ways to figure out what it is that is in you to do, how much of it you are doing, and how you can do more.

Change and Synchronicity

The essence of change embraces the notion of help or spiritual guidance from both expected and unexpected sources. Nothing happens by chance. The universe is always operating for us; we just have to recognize it.

We are all familiar with the idea of cause and effect. When we make an appointment with someone, we expect to meet that person. We are also familiar with coincidence. We think of a friend and there he is in the parking lot. Another idea, which falls somewhere between cause and effect and coincidence, is that seemingly unconnected events turn out to be connected to bring some benefit to us. Carl Jung (1971/1953) introduced this idea and called it *synchronicity*. Much later, physicists described the underlying connectedness of what appears to be chaos.

In what has been called "chaos theory" or "complexity theory," seemingly unconnected events are connected. Small events in one location cause large effects in remote areas. The classic illustration of this theory is the possible relationship between the fluttering of a butterfly's wings in the Amazon jungle with the storm in a city near you. The events appear to be unconnected, random occurrences, but we can question whether

In making changes in jobs or occupations, you have to be open to the opportunities around you, however they present themselves.

there is randomness. What appeared to be random yesterday, we have discovered, may not have been random at all. In our ordinary expectations, a small change produces a small and easily recognizable effect. But, according to chaos theory, complex relationships are better explained when one accepts that small differences in causes can lead to wildly differing results.

We can see synchronicity operating in this chapter when Allison met the boy on the bus. He turned out to be the messenger she needed at that moment, her wise person. His offhand remarks enabled her to pursue the career she sought and to deal with both aging and change effectively. His chance remarks brought together her need to separate from Steven, her admiration of Shirley's career, and her casual sighting of the ad in the newspaper. These seemingly unconnected—chaotic—events were really connected for Allison.

In making changes in jobs or occupations, you have to be open to the opportunities around you, however they present themselves. The person who has been let go or the person who is experiencing dissatisfaction is looking for the opportunities to change. However, even when we are not thinking about change, change may be suggested to us by what appear to be

We are rooted to abundance through our first energy center.
All that we need is available if only we open our eyes to see it.

random events. The unexpected meeting, the newspaper ad that seems written just for you, the chance remark from another person may all be triggers for change. Be aware of the many messages sent to you by the universe and choose from among the richness of opportunities out there.

The understanding of the beneficence of the universe brings us back full circle to the beginning of this chapter. We are rooted to abundance through our first energy center. All that we need is available if only we open our eyes to see it.

Change and Spirituality—
Some Concluding Thoughts

Meeting the challenges of life in productive ways often requires us to abandon old, tightly held images. We fear letting go of the material and letting go of the familiar. To make job or other major changes, we must trust both in ourselves and in the world around us. We go deep into ourselves to find the strength to

Spirituality is the ability to find communion with that which is the deepest within ourselves and the greatest outside ourselves.

make changes. We jump off the diving board of the familiar and trust that the water of the new will be there to embrace us. Spirituality is the ability to find communion with that which is the deepest within ourselves and the greatest outside ourselves. Trust in ourselves and trust in the universe are the essential elements of change and of spirituality.

Applications

In the story and reflections we explored the theme of change. The applications that follow are designed to help you in three ways:

- To value the age you are, without fear of moving forward with new ideas toward new experiences

- To appreciate the roots and strengths you have developed over time and through life's experiences

- To become aware of messages from expected and unexpected sources or to be open to synchronicity

Application 1: Your Tree of Life

Self-understanding is essential for productive change. Looking at your life from your earliest years to the present is a way of understanding yourself. In this application, you will use the image of a tree to represent you and your life. By drawing the tree and answering the questions about it, you will gain understanding of aspects of your life that are often overlooked. You will see how your roots developed and how to continue to nourish your own growth.

Directions: Get a piece of paper and a pencil, crayons, or markers. Draw a tree that represents your life. Look at the tree and add to the picture any elements that nourished the tree and helped it to grow when it was young. These may be represented by the sun or rain or anything else that makes sense to you. Finally, look at the tree and add any leaves or fruit the tree might bear. Then examine the tree and answer the questions that follow. Remember that the tree represents your life.

Your Tree of Life

---

1. In what kind of soil was the tree planted?

2. In what kind of soil did the tree grow to maturity?

3. Are the tree's roots deep or shallow?

4. What happened to the tree if it was ever transplanted?

5. What kind of nourishment did the tree receive in its youth?

6. What kind of nourishment does the tree need now?

7. What kind of fruit does the tree bear?

8. What kind of nourishment is needed to bear better or more plentiful fruit?

9. What would happen if the tree were transplanted today?

10. How can the tree best survive?

11. What did you learn from drawing the tree and answering the questions that you find useful in making changes in your life today?

12. What did you learn from drawing the tree and answering the questions about the strengths you will need to make changes in your life?

Application 2: Your Roots, Your Strengths

Your ability to make the changes you want depends upon your strengths. It is often difficult to recognize and acknowledge your own strengths. Sometimes it feels like bragging. However, by looking at successes in your life, you can identify your own strengths.

Everyone has strengths of varying degree in a number of areas. These are some of the areas:

■ *Physical strength*—the ability to use your body in ways that are satisfactory and rewarding to you

■ *Interpersonal strength*—the ability to work well with others and help them work with each other

■ *Emotional strength*—the ability to keep yourself together in trying circumstances

■ *Verbal strength*—the ability to express yourself clearly in speech and writing

■ *Analytic strength*—the ability to reason or to understand how the parts of a subject are interrelated

■ *Moral strength*—the ability to recognize the right thing to do, and to do it

Directions: Examine your life at three periods, at least five years apart. Using the worksheets that follow, for each period tell a story of some success you had. The success could have been one that came easily or one that was filled with difficulty. The success may have been seen by others or it may have been private. The success may even have been the overcoming of some initial failure. After you complete each story, fill in its corresponding Strength Assessment chart. Finally, complete "A Summary of My Strengths" to see how your strengths may be of use in your current and future work.

Success Story 1
Date of the story:
Now complete Strength Assessment 1.

Strength Assessment 1

Find your strengths in Success Story 1.

My physical strengths:

My interpersonal strengths:

My emotional strengths:

My verbal strengths:

My analytic strengths:

My moral strengths:

How my strengths relate to my work:

Success Story 2
Date of the story: *Now complete Strength Assessment 2.*

Strength Assessment 2

Find your strengths in Success Story 2.

My physical strengths:

My interpersonal strengths:

My emotional strengths:

My verbal strengths:

My analytic strengths:

My moral strengths:

How my strengths relate to my work:

Success Story 3

Date of the story:

Now complete Strength Assessment 3.

Strength Assessment 3

Find your strengths in Success Story 3.

My physical strengths:

My interpersonal strengths:

My emotional strengths:

My verbal strengths:

My analytic strengths:

My moral strengths:

How my strengths relate to my work:

Directions: Now complete the summary of your strengths. Consider whether you are using all your strengths today and how you might use them in the future in your work or other aspects of your life.

A Summary of My Strengths

Strength	In Which Stories	Current Use	Future Use
Physical:			
Interpersonal:			
Emotional:			
Verbal:			
Analytic:			
Moral:			
Others:			

29

Application 3: A Meditation on Precious Days

Directions: You may want to ask someone else to read this slowly to you, or you may want to read the meditation into a tape recorder for yourself before you begin.

Sit in a comfortable chair with a firm back, or on the floor with your back straight and your legs crossed comfortably. Place your hands on your thighs, palms up and slightly open. Straighten yourself as if you were about to pay attention. Now let your shoulders drop naturally. Breathe slowly in through your nose and out through your mouth. You may make a sound with your breath as you exhale. That's fine. Just breathe in and out deeply and evenly for a few moments. Let your breath return to normal.

Begin to feel the power of the earth wherever your body is in contact with the floor or chair. Maintain your contact with the abundant power of the physical, material world. Let the energy of the brown and red earth, its dryness, its moist fertility enter your body. Keep the earth's energy within you. At the same time, become aware of the top of your head. Imagine you can feel the electricity of all the spirit in the cosmos. As you draw in one breath, draw in the abundance of the earth. Exhale. As you draw in the next breath, draw in the light of the cosmos. Picture this as you breathe in and out. Any time you lose your concentration in the exercise, just return to your breathing.

Turn your attention to the base of your spine. This is the location of your first energy center. It grounds you and connects you to the material abundance of the universe. The energy center is a red disk. Begin to spin the red disk by breathing in and out of it. Breathe in and out of the red disk and feel your connection to the best place on earth for you, a place that is calm and quiet, a place where you are quite comfortable being alone. Perhaps it is a green meadow near a brook. Maybe it is in a forest as the leaves begin to sprout in early spring or as they begin to turn and fall in autumn. Your safe place may be near a shore where you hear and see the rhythm of the waves. It may be a riverbank. Your safe place may be indoors—a room at your grandparents' that you loved as a child, or an imaginary room you have dreamed of. There is no one place for all. Find your safe place. Try to make it as real as you can in your mind's eye. Find the colors in it. Hear the sounds or music or silence. Smell the air. Feel the textures under your feet or in your fingertips. Relax in your safe haven. Spend a few minutes looking around. While you are here, a guide may appear to you. It may be an animal or a person, a real figure, a historical one, or someone or something completely imaginary. This is a very safe place for you, and your guide is there only to help you. Your guide will appear if you need a guide. Your guide cares for you unconditionally. Relaxed in your safe haven, you are now ready to affirm the preciousness of this moment, the day, the time, the year that is now.

Say the following four sentences to yourself four times:

I am in the perfect place at the perfect time for me.
I am the perfect age to do what I want to do right now.
I trust in the abundance of the universe to meet all of
    my needs.
I am precious. This time is precious.

When you are ready, slowly open your eyes.

Application 4: In Your Own Voice

Directions: You are going to keep a journal to help you become more aware of the messages that come to you, regardless of their source. Acquire a notebook that you will use only for this journal. Select one that appeals to you. Perhaps you like a notebook with a black-and-white marbleized cover and lined paper, the kind you may have used when you first began school. Maybe you want a notebook with colored sheets in a shade you really like. There is only one quality you should definitely seek in the notebook: Choose one whose pages cannot be torn out. There are no "mistakes" in a journal. There are only "correct" answers. What may seem like a mistake today may turn out to be one of the most meaningful ideas you've recorded. Recording and retaining the journal leaves you open to the synchronicity of your own life.

Begin the journal by noting your thoughts on the story of Allison and the reflections in this chapter. Be aware of any changes you are making or would like to make in your own life. These may be internal changes or changes in the world around you. Use any style of writing you like. Write as much or as little as you would like. If you don't like the way the story of Allison began or ended, change it. Then think about what the changes in the story mean for Allison and for you.

If you have reflections from books you've read, songs you've heard, or other sources, record them in the journal as well. On a daily basis, or as close to it as you can come, note any words you have heard that resonate with meaning for you. You too may meet a stranger on a bus. You may hear something from a family member, friend, or colleague. A song, a movie, a television program, or a book may have a line or more that just strikes you. Record it. If you would like, write down any thoughts about the line. But if you have no thoughts about it at the moment, write the words down anyway.

From time to time, but no less than once a month, reread your journal. Look for connections among voices, ideas, and your evolving career.

Balance

Helen on the High Wire

The Story

Helen hurriedly wrapped the Victorian candlesticks for her customer and glanced surreptitiously at her watch. At the same time as she thought about supper for Eddy and the kids, she asked politely, "Is there anything more I can help you with?"

Thankful for once for the failure to sell any more antiques, Helen closed the door behind the customer and rushed to shut off the lights, set the alarm, and lock up. She ran to the parking lot, jumped into her beat-up Hyundai and, slowing only for lights and traffic, raced to the supermarket. She headed for the veggie aisle, sighing—she had to put out a salad and some green vegetable, even if only to show the kids what they should be eating. At least Matthew, the football hero of Pacific High, had come around to eating balanced meals. But Mark was still into junior high junk food, and Nancy, her ten-year-old baby, had always been a fussy eater. Next stop was the bread aisle for the hero rolls. Thank goodness she'd already made a sauce for the sloppy joes.

Helen pulled into her driveway just as Nancy's after-school group bus pulled up. At least she had made it home in time. Mark soon followed on his bike, and Matthew would be there any minute, getting a lift from one of his friends. That meant she could serve dinner as soon as Eddy got home. He liked to have dinner ready as soon as he came home. She could no longer remember why he wanted dinner on the table the minute he walked in. She couldn't remember why she had honored that request—if it had ever been a request—when they were first married. And she certainly did not know why she felt she had to do it now. Setting the table, she sighed. There were so many things she just felt she had to do.

"Hey, you kids, turn off the TV and get washed. Dinner's almost ready."

"Okay, just a minute, Mom," Mark called back.

And Nancy echoed with, "Yeah, just a minute. This program's almost over."

Nothing happened. Helen heard Matthew's friends pull up and pull out, depositing him in the driveway. "Hi, Mom." He gave her a quick hug and crashed on the living room couch with his brother and sister.

"C'mon, kids, you've already had first call. No more TV now. No more TV until after homework. And get washed. Daddy will be here any minute."

The change in sound from the cartoon's rap music background to running water told Helen that she had been successful. Another sound, the pickup in the driveway, let her know that Eddy was home. He grunted his way through the kitchen, mumbled something about a quick shower, and disappeared up the stairs. Helen sighed, tossed the salad, and cut the rolls.

Dinner over, Mark cleared the table while Matthew loaded the dishwasher and Nancy washed the two pots. At least, Helen thought, I have finally gotten the kids to assume some responsibility around here. Although I still do all the laundry and cook and clean the house and run that damn antique store for Mrs. Marsh.

Eddy was, of course, hunkered down over the papers he had spread across the dining room table as soon as it had been cleared. Helen heard the kids go to their rooms. She waited a few minutes and then went to check that homework was really on their agenda. Satisfied, she sat down across the table from Eddy.

"Did you have enough to eat?" she asked.

"It was okay. I wasn't very hungry."

"Do you want anything else?"

"Can't you see I'm working here? If I don't get these bids in for the construction on the Murphy job, there may very well not be any suppers anymore."

Even though Helen knew she should just shut up, she could not resist saying, "You know, you're not the only one working for the family."

"Ha ha," he gave his usual fake laugh. "If we had to survive on your 'antiquee shoppee' earnings, we'd be eating the same kind of junk you sell."

Helen sighed once more and slipped out of the room into the now darkened living room. She sat on the couch and thought about all the things she and Eddy didn't say to each other. She couldn't tell him about her job and what she liked and didn't like. If she said what she liked, he would just make fun of her. And if she said what she didn't like, he would just tell her to quit. She deliberately turned her mind to what she had to do for tomorrow. She clicked her mental list through breakfast, making the kids' lunches, straightening up, and then the store. She had to open by eleven in the morning, which meant getting in by ten to do the books and billing. At least she would be out by four, in time to make dinner.

Eddy left early the next morning. His regular early departure was one of life's few blessings. The kids got off with no more than the usual fuss, and she actually got to the store before ten. Helen looked around the shop. She saw the burnished metals of old lamps and the enameled china designs.

These objects and others were what had first brought her to Marsh's Antiques.

She had not had the money to buy anything, but she loved to walk by the shop with each of her kids and look at the window display. Just five years earlier, when Nancy had started school, Helen had begun to wander into Marsh's. Mrs. Marsh had seen her interest and begun talking to her. This had eventually led to the part-time selling job that Helen had loved. Of course, it had taken a lot of persuasion to get Eddy to agree that she could take the job. She had to promise him that absolutely nothing would change at home. She would still do everything for him and the kids, and, of course, she realized he had to believe that the money would make no difference in their lives.

Now Mrs. Marsh, poor old Mrs. Marsh, could barely make it into the shop herself. Arthritis had just about done in her knees. She tried to spend most of her time in warm, sunny places—Florida, the Caribbean. But that meant that Mrs. Marsh had come to rely more and more on Helen, who felt good to be trusted with running the whole show—buying, evaluating, pricing, selling, and keeping all the records. Along with the additional responsibilities had come a nice raise in pay, but also a not-so-nice increase in the amount of time taken from Helen's day. Helen realized that antiques used to be a release, fun for her. Now the store was the same kind of responsibility as home. Her responsibility.

One more day in the store went by. Helen locked up. The only difference between today and yesterday was the need to go to the dry cleaners instead of the supermarket. The routine continued. Car, home, greet kids, begin supper. Once again, Matthew was the last kid to come home. But this time, there was no "hi, Mom" and hug. Nor did Matthew go into the living room with Mark and Nancy. He walked slowly up the stairs, and Helen heard his door close.

Helen heard nothing more and, after ten minutes, began to worry. Matthew was rarely so quiet for so long. She walked up the stairs listening for a clue. She didn't hear Matthew's music or his voice on the telephone. Helen knocked on his door.

"Yeah?" said Matthew.

"Can I come in? It's Mom."

"Well, what a surprise! Okay, I guess so."

Helen found Matthew lying on his bed with his hands behind his head. "What's the matter, Hon? Is something wrong?" she asked.

"Oh just some stupid school stuff."

"Well, do you want to tell me about it?"

"You probably wouldn't understand."

"Try me."

"It's not important. Just forget about it."

"It may not be important to you. But it's important to me because whatever it is seems to be making you unhappy. C'mon. You can tell your old Mom."

"We didn't have history today. Instead, remember that special test I told you about last week, the one about what I should do when I finish school? Well, the counselor came into class today and explained about how to read our results. And the highest number tells you what you should do. It said I should be a lawyer or politician. I don't want to do that. I want to work with Dad. He said I could come into his business and he would call it Dombey and Son once I finished my education. I don't want to do what I don't want to do."

Helen looked lovingly at Matthew. "Matthew," Helen said as emphatically as she could, "I don't want you ever to have to do work you don't want to do. You can be free to choose, not like me."

"What do you mean, Mom? Don't you like being our Mom?"

"Of course, I love being your Mom. But there's more to me than just my 'momness.'"

"Don't you like working in the store, as Dad calls it, the 'antiquee shoppee'?"

"Yes, I do. But there it's not as clear. I like the parts where I work with the antiques, but I don't like the paperwork. You know, if I took one of those tests, I bet it would show that I should be a restorer of old paintings. I saw a show on public television about that kind of work in a museum, and that's what I'd like to do."

"Mom, that would be great. But I just don't get it. You're a grown-up. No one can tell you what to do. And I love you, Mom, and I don't want you ever to do work you don't want to do. Unless you don't want to make me supper." And with that Matthew bounded off the bed and down the stairs.

Helen remained, thinking. What a surprise that Eddy had spoken to Matthew about the future. She didn't think Eddy ever spoke to anyone in the family. And what a wonderful man her son was turning out to be. How loving. But what about herself? She was a grown-up. When was she going to take hold of herself, without giving up the others? Maybe she could find a way. That's what she would think about tonight after dinner.

Career Issues

In the story, Helen faced three major questions:

▌ How can she balance her two work roles—the paid role in the antique shop and the unpaid role of wife and mother?

▌ How can she admit to herself that her aspirations are different from the traditional role she has played?

▌ How can she balance her desire to change her career direction with her need to conceal any dissatisfaction from her husband?

Here are some related career issues that many people face:

▌ Recognizing the challenges that face dual-career couples

▌ Recognizing the challenges that come from varied life roles

▌ Knowing how to use time for greatest satisfaction

▌ Understanding that living in changing times creates tensions between traditional expectations and contemporary realities

▌ Achieving the spiritual balance that helps create a wholeness in our life work

Reflections

The world is full of seemingly opposing forces, or dualities. We see black and white, winter and summer, male and female, or in Eastern terms, the yin and the yang. Yet each side of the pair of apparent opposites could not exist as an opposite without its partner. The two make one. Balance is the ability to hold an image in which the two sides of any pair are equal to each other such that they make a circle.

But balance in life is not simply a matter of thought. To maintain balance we must have action. We find balance through a series of movements that keep us centered among the alternatives facing us. Do you remember riding the seesaw when you were a child? First you had the high of being on top—sometimes a bit scary. Then you came down with a bump. Eventually you and your partner figured out how to stay just in the middle. But if you tried to stay there without moving at all, you soon found that impossible. You could only keep the seesaw balanced by making a series of continuing adjustments of your weight on your end of the seesaw and of your playmate's on the opposite end. When you were a little older and learned to drive, one of

Balance in life is not simply a matter of thought.
To maintain balance we must have action.

the first goals was to steer the car down a street or lane without veering from right to left. At first you may have tried to do that by holding the steering wheel completely steady. If you held the wheel steady for more than a moment or two, you soon ran off the road. As the wheels of the car encountered the uneven surface of the road or differences in the bank of the road, you saw that to stay centered you had to keep making adjustments. So it is in life, balance requires action. Even in this concept the reverse is also true, action produces balance. As Eric Hoffer (1955) wrote, "Action is at bottom a swinging and flailing of the arms to regain one's balance and keep afloat."

You read earlier about the center of energy near the base of your spine and its connections to the roots of the material world. The energy center, or chakra, that is associated with balance is the second chakra, which is located in the pelvic area. This location suggests that the chakra is about sexual energy, and it is. Sexual energy includes not only procreation and the pleasures of sexuality but two other essential spiritual concepts. The first is fertility, creativity in its most general sense. The second is the innate maleness and femaleness within all living things.

The circle for the second chakra is the circle that contains the yin and the yang. Neither is complete without the balance of the other. This concept is not unique to Eastern thought. It is at the heart of the creation story of Genesis. "And God created humans in God's own image. In the image of God, the creator created them, male and female." The implication is that God in the Judeo-Christian tradition encompasses both male and female since God is the essence of existence. And this essence of existence we may also call *spirit*.

Each of us includes this spirit, this essence of existence. At the same time, the events of our daily lives challenge our very being. We struggle to maintain our balance against these challenges. The central theme of balance is illustrated in the story of

Each of us seeks balance in our relationship with others, balance in our relationship to the circumstances in our lives, and most important, balance within ourselves.

Helen, Eddy, and their children. Helen and Eddy are struggling for balance in their marriage roles, balance within their own careers, and balance between their own needs and the needs of the others in the family. By looking at the challenges facing Helen and Eddy, we can see how issues of balance play out in daily life. While your situation may be different in its particulars, understanding how Helen's family may rebalance their lives will also provide ideas for you. Each of us seeks balance in our relationship with others, balance in our relationship to the circumstances in our lives, and most important, balance within ourselves. These are the major sections in this set of reflections:

■ Balance in our Relationship with Others

■ Balance in Our Relationship to Circumstance

■ Balance Within Ourselves

Balance in Our Relationship with Others

First, let's look at the issues facing Helen and Eddy as a couple. Their struggles play out in the context of a traditional marriage in a world where external circumstances threaten to negate those very traditions. Helen and Eddy are caught in routines of behavior predetermined by social roles they have accepted without question or reflection. For instance, Eddy is the head of the household and primary provider for the family. Dinner must be served when he wants it served even though Helen is now also working and no longer at home during the day to tend to this preparation. Eddy is neither a bad guy nor a deadbeat. He and Helen are following routines that have been part of traditional family schedules for many generations. Indeed, that may be the problem. The world has changed dramatically over the last several generations. In general, men no longer go into the field, the factory, or the office while women work at home scrubbing clothes on rocks, soaking them in tubs, or even throwing them in the automatic washer. Generally now, both men and women leave home for other work sites. When men went out to work and women's work was centered in the home, it probably made sense for the woman to adjust her schedule to the man's. She undoubtedly had hard work to do, particularly without modern conveniences, but the timing of that work was more flexible than the timing of the arrival of the husband from his labors. Economic changes, as well as changes in education patterns and changes in what women expect of themselves, make the two-wage-earner family more common than in the past. In other words, Eddy may scoff at his wife's job, but in order to have what they want, Helen has to work.

The dual-career family puts stress on everybody. The husband may feel diminished by having to depend on his wife. The wife, on the other hand, may feel overburdened and tired because she has accepted a wage-earning role while not relinquishing any control over the management of the household. One young woman we know, for example, earns in excess of a quarter of a million dollars a year as a corporate officer of a major drug company. Her husband works at home as a computer

The dual-career family puts stress on everybody.

graphics designer. Nevertheless, it is this wife who plans the meals, does the shopping, and sees to all that is needed for the children to get to school and home again safely. While the husband is perfectly willing to help, the direction still comes from the wife, and all of the work of the home is seen as hers by both of them.

You can see that the pull of traditional roles operates whether a family is well-to-do or just making it. The well-to-do family has more options since they can hire help with some tasks. However, all couples need to seek balance in their roles through deliberate sharing. Deliberate sharing cannot take place without talking. While Eddy and Helen do not appear to battle, they also do not communicate. There is neither discord nor discourse on the real issues. The importance of dialogue is described by Peter Senge (1990) when he talks about the "learning organization." In dialogue, people seek solutions together instead of coming together to convince others of some idea they already had or some position they already support. For example, Helen and Eddy need to explore their entire approach to the use of time—time on the job, time running the home, time spent with each other, time for the children, and time for themselves as individuals. A learning organization is one that is capable of growing to meet ever-changing circumstances. A healthy family is an example of a learning organization.

While Matthew, the oldest child in Helen's story, is at the culturally accepted point of career choice—in the junior or senior year of high school—his mother continues to be making career decisions. This is another critical aspect of balance in the family. Our children need to see us as stable and unchanging. Matthew is worried when he asks, "Don't you like being our Mom?" Yet we know that changing economic circumstances,

The ability of the adults to engage in frank discussion often spells the difference between dysfunction and balance within the family.

the growth of technology in all industries, and longer productive work lives mean that each of us is likely to have four or more changes in occupational direction, not just changes of job. As parents, we must balance our own need for change with our presentation of stability for our children.

These issues become even more complicated when there are issues of divorce, separation, and blended families. While this is the stuff of which television situation comedies are often made, the situations are not simple when faced in real life. Nevertheless, it is possible to find balance. The process of dialogue described earlier becomes even more essential. The ability of the adults to engage in frank discussion often spells the difference between dysfunction and balance within the family.

Balance in Our Relationship to Circumstance

Many of the issues that we just discussed in the context of balance between ourselves and others are also issues of balance between ourselves and circumstance. In real life, the two—others and circumstance—can rarely be separated. However, for clearer understanding, let's pull out the issues of circumstance and examine them.

The time in which we live is a matter of circumstance. You noticed earlier that Helen and Eddy were trying to live traditional lives in changing times. We are all influenced by the values of the time in which we live. Furthermore, since our parents raised us to "do the right thing," we are influenced by the values of the time in which they lived, and of course, they in turn were

Life is a difficult juggling act. Balance is hard to find.

influenced by their parents, and so tradition becomes ingrained in our minds. These traditions can be helpful or can impede our ability to respond to challenges to our balance in the here and now.

Life is a difficult juggling act. Balance is hard to find. Picture three balloons. One is self, a second is other, and the third is circumstance. These balloons are not filled equally, and what is more, at any given moment their relative sizes change. You can see the problem in keeping them in the air. But the problem of finding balance in real life is even more complicated. Not only are the balloons unequally and unsteadily inflated, they are interlocked. The poet Unamuno (1952) suggested that a person cannot be separated from his or her circumstances in life. And circumstances always involve others.

Often it appears that the easier way to achieve balance would be to change someone else or some circumstances. For example, you may be finding that you don't get along as well as you would

The most productive change is the change you bring about in yourself.

like with your teenage children. The temptation is to focus on how to change them. Why won't they speak freely at dinner with shining-faced smiles as they did when they were five, you ask. You're unhappy at work because there is too much competition in your office. You try to convince your boss to reassign some folks. Maybe that nuisance will just quit, go away! That would change your circumstances. Most often, however, strategies to change our circumstances fail. The most productive change is the change you bring about in yourself. After all, you have more control over yourself than over anyone or anything else.

And often the payoff is that by controlling yourself, your interaction with others will change them.

Here are four common ways in which effective personal change takes place. You may find some suggestions useful to you for changing yourself to bring about better balance in your life.

- *Change your view of time.* Time is neither infinite nor scarce. We simply have the time of our lives. This means, for some people, stop procrastinating. Get with it now. You may never have the chance later. For others it means slow down. Enjoy the experience of the moment. This moment will never come again.

- *Change your view of authority.* Who is the authority in your life? Do you listen to your own understandings of what to do and when to do it, or are you directed by others around you? Are you driven (as Helen was) by unexamined expectations from the culture in which you were raised? Sometimes we have a parent within us who tells us what we "should" do, and we listen to that voice without question. At other times, we have a child rebelling against that parent, telling us to do things we want to do whether or not they are now appropriate to our best interests as adults. Stop and listen to your inner voices.

- *Change your behavior and you'll change what you think.* A couple was having difficulty getting along in day-to-day behaviors. Each felt the other was master of the "put-down." From conversation, it became clear that not only was there a strong bond of love between the couple, but neither actually wanted to hurt the other. The couple arrived at the idea of addressing each other by terms of endearment whenever the wrangling seemed about to set in. Just saying "dear," "darling," "sweetheart," or "honey" before the most ordinary sentences led to increased harmony, indeed often to the wonderful laughter of understanding between longtime friends.

- *Change your self-talk.* Many messages we give ourselves are negative. "I can't do that." "I can't do anything right." "I'm stupid."

There is an entire school of psychotherapy based on the concept that what we say to ourselves about ourselves affects how we feel about ourselves. It's not the other way around. You don't say cruel things to yourself because you feel bad. You feel bad because you have made hurtful judgments about your own performance and abilities. We often are much harder on ourselves in our self-talk than we would ever be to another person. You know that you will get more cooperation from someone else by praising that person. Try it on yourself.

Balance Within Ourselves

Helen and Eddy face issues of balance in their relationship with each other and balance of themselves and their circumstances. But, of course, they can't speak about these issues because they have not each found the balance within themselves. Let's look at Helen in particular because we know more about her. Helen knows what she likes to do in the antique store—work with the antiques; and she knows what she doesn't like—the bookkeeping and ordering. She also knows what she would eventually like to do—restore old paintings. But she does not see herself as free to do what she wants either right now or in the future. She feels her life is determined by her responsibilities to others. While it is true that some of these responsibilities, as we said, are culturally supported, others, such as her taking over for Mrs. Marsh, are individually driven. In sum, because she doesn't see herself as free, she isn't free. This lack of freedom restricts her motion. As we have seen, motion is essential for balance.

Helen was awakened to the lack of balance in her life through the words of her son, "You're a grown-up. No one can tell you what to do. And I love you, Mom, and I don't want you ever to do work you don't want to do." For Helen, her son was the wise person who brought her the moment of enlightenment. He understood that it was just as important for her to find her way as it was for him to find his. What surprised him was that she had not done so. However, many people do work that they don't want to do. This work, not by its nature, but by its lack of personal appeal, puts us off-kilter, out of balance. May Sarton (1965) wrote, "The woman who needs to create works of art is born with a kind of psychic tension in her which drives her unmercifully to find a way to balance, to make herself whole. Every human being has this need." Doing the work we want to do, whether this work is defined by the outside world as art or not, is what inspirits us.

One of the aspects of work that pleases most people is the variety they find in their job regardless of how structured the job may seem to an outsider. Wuthnow (1996) conducted a survey that examined the attitudes toward work of 2,000 adult American workers. He found that the respondents frequently discussed how important variety on the job was to them. A detailed analysis of what they reported, however, also showed that this variety was made up of many small differences in daily routines rather than large swings from one kind of task to something completely different. Helen wanted variety but reported that her life was too routine. She did not see what she had. She worked with numbers

One of the aspects of work that pleases most people is the variety they find in their job regardless of how structured the job may seem to an outsider.

in preparing the books and ordering. She worked with objects in the store. She worked with people in sales and in her family. And her responsibilities ranged from childcare to store management. There is infinite variety in life if we stop and notice it.

Often we get confused between job and career. We tell ourselves that our jobs are our careers. What is more, we tell ourselves that our jobs are who we are. Donald Super (1980) told us that our career is far more than our job. It is, in fact, all the roles we play in the life space that is allotted to us. These roles include:

- Student

- Child

- Spouse

- Homemaker

- Parent

- Citizen

- Person who enjoys leisure activities

- Worker

These roles are not time-limited. We can be both parent and child at the same time in life. We can be students at any age, not just the ages of five through twenty-two. And we can move in and out of being a worker for pay and still have a career.

Sometimes you may find yourself in more than one job at a time. As more and more businesses move away from a large, permanent, full-time workforce, more and more workers are engaged in contract work. Contract work may be full time or part time at any given moment. But by its nature it is not and will not be full time "forever." That means you need to be aware of all the skills and knowledge you possess so that you are ready to move not only from one job to another but to balance time among them. A second or third opportunity may come along before you have finished the first. In our story, Helen already illustrated what Charles Handy (1989) called the "portfolio career." Just as

Sometimes you may find yourself in more than one job at a time. As more and more businesses move away from a large, permanent, full-time workforce, more and more workers are engaged in contract work.

an artist has a portfolio of different works, so does the individual keep a portfolio in her or his head of different work that can be done. Helen, whether she recognized it or not, had all the skills she had developed both at home and in the antique shop to bring to her subsequent money-earning efforts. Remember that in today's world, security resides within you, not in your relationship with a particular employer.

The allocation of time and space for the roles within our careers is another matter of balance. Consider how you spend your time in carrying out any of the roles of current interest to you. Stephen Covey, author of *Seven Habits of Highly Effective People* (1989), looked at how we balance time in another way. He proposed that all tasks fall into one of four categories:

- Important and urgent

- Important but not urgent

- Not important but urgent

- Neither important nor urgent

Covey suggested that all of our time be spent on tasks that fall into the first two categories, that is, tasks that are important to us. Tasks that appear urgent but are not important are often the worst wasters of our time. We are impelled, often by the voices of others, to do things that we do not value but that have somehow taken on an urgency of their own. Sorting the tasks that face you brings you back to earlier considerations raised in this chapter.

We are impelled, often by the voices of others, to do things that we do not value but that have somehow taken on an urgency of their own.

You cannot figure out what is important until you recognize the relative values of all the roles you play and of how and when you play them. Similarly, you cannot figure out what is important to you until you recognize whose voice you are obeying.

Balance and Spirituality— Some Concluding Thoughts

Experiencing ourselves as fully human includes knowing our own maleness and femaleness. It is internal and does not depend on carrying out socially defined roles. Jung (1933/1931) said that there is femaleness and maleness within each of us. This maleness and femaleness is depicted as the yin and yang mentioned earlier. And the yin and yang stand for all seeming opposites. As we discover ourselves as mature individuals, we learn to balance

Experiencing ourselves as fully human includes knowing our own maleness and femaleness.

or reconcile the seeming dualities within us and in this way we experience the wholeness of ourselves. This sense of wholeness is the experience of our spirit. And this sense of wholeness connects us to ongoing creation.

Two millennia ago, the rabbi Hillel (1945/c. 1st century BCE) gave us three essential questions of balance to ask ourselves: "If I am not for myself, who will be for me?" "If I am only for myself, what am I?" "If not now, when?" So Hillel taught us to be balanced in our concern for ourselves and others. And when he said, "If not now, when?" he taught us that the balance we seek to achieve is only possible through action in this world at this time.

Applications

In this chapter we looked at the importance of balance and challenges to balance from the external and internal sources. We also looked at how we can meet the challenges and restore balance. The applications that follow are designed to help you in three ways:

■ To recognize the challenges in your own work and other life roles

■ To address these challenges

■ To achieve the spiritual balance that helps create a wholeness in your life

Application 1: Balancing Your Life Roles

You are going to examine the relative time you spend on each of eight life roles. The purpose of this activity is to help you assess whether this is how you want to spend your time and to consider changes you may want to make to create the balance among life roles that you consider important. The roles are (1) worker, (2) person at leisure, (3) citizen, (4) family member (parent and/or child), (5) spouse or partner, 6) friend, (7) religious or spiritual participant, and (8) learner.

There is no ideal balance that applies to everyone. The idea is to find the balance that suits your values.

Directions: Look at the following diagram: Each of the eight life roles is represented at the end of the intersecting lines. Consider how much time you spend on each role relative to the others. Put an *x* at the spot on each line that indicates the amount of time you spend on that life role. Connect the *x*'s.

Examine the figure you have created. Does it seem accurate? In other words, does it show how you spend your time? If not, correct your drawing.

Now consider whether this is how you want to spend your time. If you would like to change some of the balance among your life roles, put a small circle at the spot on the lines that represents how you would like to spend your time. If you want to spend about the same amount of time on a particular role, just put the circle in the same spot as the *x*. Now connect the circles.

What would you have to do to make the changes in your life so that you spend your time in a way that gives you greater satisfaction in your varied life roles? You might want to enter any reflections in your journal.

Balancing Your Life Roles

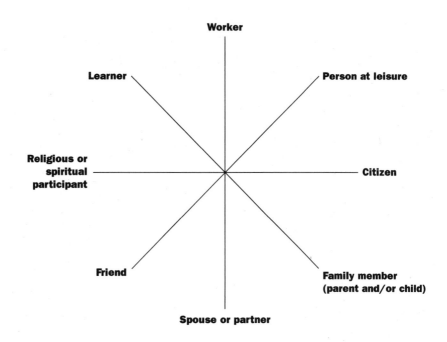

Application 2: Balancing Your Balloons

In life we are always trying to balance our own needs and desires with the demands of others and the pressures of circumstance. Picture these as three helium-filled balloons you are holding together at the bottom of their long strings. One balloon is your own desires. The second balloon is the demands that others make upon you. And the third balloon is the circumstances in which you find yourself. You would like to keep those balloons balanced and under control. But when the wind blows, the balloons bump against each other. Sometimes the strings get tangled and it seems you will never be able to separate one from the other.

Directions: Four sets of balloons are pictured on page 55. In the first set, the balloons are balanced. In the second set, the balloon of self dominates the demands of others and the circumstances. In the third set, the demands of others overwhelm the self and circumstances. And in the fourth set, the circumstances are prominent.

Examine the balloons and answer the questions on the corresponding worksheet on page 56, "Can You Balance Your Balloons?"

Balancing Your Balloons

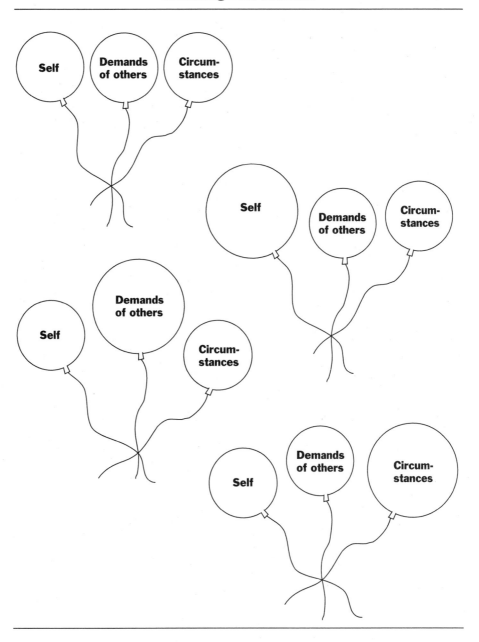

Can You Balance Your Balloons?

---

1. Which set of balloons represents your life now?

2. If your balloons are not in balance, what would you have to change to bring them into balance?

3. *Warning: The winds always blow.* The balance is unsteady. What inner strength do you need to develop or draw upon to keep the balloons balanced?

Application 3: Hearing Voices

Early life experiences are often recorded as voices within our heads. We replay them, sometimes unconsciously, as if they were our own personal instructional videos. We can only decide the relevance of the voices to our adult lives by bringing the dialogues to awareness.

Directions: In the spaces below, write three warnings from your parents that you keep hearing in your head. Then consider how these warnings keep you in balance or keep you from being in balance by answering the five questions about the place of the warning in your life today. Finally, decide whether your parental voice should keep saying the same thing or whether you want to change it to better fit the circumstances of your life today.

For example, all children who grew up in the northeastern United States repeatedly heard, "Don't go swimming before July 1st or after August 31st." Many then moved to other parts of the country or the world and learned, if they dared to try it, that the difference in water or air temperature that lay behind the injunction did not apply in their new circumstances. Of course, some who moved never thought about the meaning of the warning and never tried swimming at other times. They might change the warning to read, "Don't go swimming when the water or air feels too cold for your comfort unless you are wearing a wet suit."

Hearing Voices

Parental Warning 1: _____

Does this warning still operate in your life today?

When is it still helpful?

When is it inappropriate or harmful?

Do you want to keep hearing it?

What sentence can you substitute that will eliminate or change the warning to make it a productive thought of your own?

Parental Warning 2: _____

Does this warning still operate in your life today?

When is it still helpful?

When is it inappropriate or harmful?

Do you want to keep hearing it?

What sentence can you substitute that will eliminate or change the warning to make it a productive thought of your own?

Parental Warning 3: _____

Does this warning still operate in your life today?

When is it still helpful?

When is it inappropriate or harmful?

Do you want to keep hearing it?

What sentence can you substitute that will eliminate or change the warning to make it a productive thought of your own?

Application 4: A Meditation on Balance

Directions: You may want to ask someone else to read this slowly to you, or you may want to read the meditation into a tape recorder for yourself before you begin. This meditation begins like all the others with directions that will put you in a receptive frame of mind and spirit.

Sit in a comfortable chair with a firm back, or on the floor with your back straight and your legs crossed comfortably. Place your hands on your thighs, palms up and slightly open. Straighten yourself as if you were about to pay attention. Now let your shoulders drop naturally. Breathe slowly in through your nose and out through your mouth. You may make a sound with your breath as you exhale. That's fine. Just breathe in and out deeply and evenly for a few moments. Let your breath return to normal.

Begin to feel the power of the earth wherever your body is in contact with the floor or chair. Maintain your contact with the abundant power of the physical, material world. Let the energy of the brown and red earth, its dryness, its moist fertility enter your body. Keep the earth's energy within you. At the same time, become aware of the top of your head. Imagine you can feel the electricity of all the spirit in the cosmos. As you draw in one breath, draw in the abundance of the earth. Exhale. As you draw in the next, draw in the light of the cosmos. Picture this as you breathe in and out. Any time you lose your concentration in the exercise, just return to your breathing.

Move your attention to the first energy center, the one at the base of your spine. See the red disk spinning at that energy center. Breathe in and out of the red disk several times.

Now move your attention to your pelvis. Picture an orange disk spinning around your pelvis. This is the energy of your second energy center. Breathe into the orange disk. Spin it with your breath. As your breath expands your lungs and you begin to exhale, feel orangeness permeating your body. Feel the orange color in every cell of your body. Return your attention to the disk. Picture the orange disk as being made up of two interlocking halves. Use any image of two halves of a circle that you know. If you know the picture of the yin and yang symbols, you may want to use those. Keep the two halves of the orange circle together by the energy of your breath. Feel the perfect balance of the circle. Feel the connectedness of the two halves as they fit perfectly together. Breathe in and out of the orange disk for a few more moments. Allow your breath to become normal.

Keep your eyes closed, and repeat the following affirmations four times:

My body, mind, and spirit are in perfect balance.
I can balance all that life asks of me.
I know how to spend my time wisely.

When you are ready, slowly open your eyes.

Application 5: In Your Own Voice— Continuing Your Journal

Continue your journal by noting your thoughts on the story of Helen, Eddy, and their children. If you did not like any part of the story, you might begin by writing changes to it. Consider the reflections that followed the story. Did they raise any questions or ideas for your own use? You may also want to include ideas that came to you when you did the other applications for this chapter. Think about what balance means in your own life. Look for opportunities to recenter yourself and record these in your journal. As before, ideas about balance that you want to record in your journal may come from any source that has meaning for you. Remember to keep writing in and rereading your journal.

Energy

Bob's Barbeque

The Story

The flags were flying over the restaurant, and it seemed to Bob that the whole world had turned out for his opening day. Of course his wife was there, and his two sons with their wives, and the grandkids. He saw some people from town that he recognized but didn't know well. He saw his close friends and even his cousins, those skunks who had pushed him out of the family business.

Bob was not going to let bad memories ruin his good day. After all, it was their lack of faith in his business ability that had led to his leaving the Hanson family business of dairy product labeling. For years the Hansons had designed and manufactured the cartons and labels for cheeses, butters, and milk products of all kinds produced throughout the Midwest. But now, he remembered to forget them. He was living his life's dream—opening his own barbecue restaurant.

He knew that some people would think he was nuts to start a new business, but he felt proud that he was taking the kind of risk many a younger man would avoid. When he was squeezed out, he left with a decent pension and social security, enough to continue his modest lifestyle, but not enough to do all he wanted for his kids and to set up college funds for his grand-children. The cousins wanted him out of the business. Now he was out for good. He had liquidated his stock and sunk all the money into this restaurant. Bob knew the family was surprised. They had never seen him as much of a businessman, a risk taker, an entrepreneur. In fact, he hadn't seen himself that way either. But then there was the restaurant dream, and there was no way to realize that dream without taking charge.

"Congratulations, Bob, old buddy. This place is great."

"I love these ribs."

"And the chicken is great."

Bob thanked each of the guests as they complimented him and left the restaurant.

For the next few weeks, Bob was too busy to really pay atten-tion to the flow of business. He was still ordering stuff, arranging the tables, and placing ads in the local papers. He liked to have a slightly different ad each week and he had written down a lot of the compliments on that opening day. Each week he used a new one. "Bob's the best!" "Ribs to die for!" "That chicken will send you out cluckin'." He chortled to himself as he wrote the ads.

But when Bob completed his books after the first month, he was surprised at how much he had spent and how little he had taken in. He began to watch the flow of customers. The restau-rant could seat fifty people at once; figure two to three turnovers in an evening plus some lunches. That should mean around one hundred fifty meals a day on a good day, maybe a hundred on a slow one. The restautrant was barely serving that many meals in a week.

Bob had read up on restaurants. He knew that word of mouth was important and that it took a while for a restaurant to build a following. But how was there going to be word of mouth if too few mouths came in to talk?

Bob looked up and saw a stranger looking around his restau-rant. "Care to have a seat?" Bob asked him.

"No sir," the stranger held out his hand. "My name's Gary White. And I'm here to help you. I see you have a new restaurant, and my guess is that it's not doing very well."

"What makes you say that?"

"Well, I can see that you want this to be a barbecue place, but it just doesn't have the right feel. Barbecue to most people goes with red. Red is barbecue if you know what I mean. What you need is red tablecloths and napkins."

Bob was skeptical. But he wasn't doing the business he had expected to do. Maybe the guy was right.

Gary took out his order book and said, "I have a special price for you, just for new businesses." Bob placed an order for red cloths and paper napkins and bibs.

The business seemed to pick up for a week, but maybe it was just the cheeriness of the red that made Bob feel better. When he did the books, he still saw only red ink there too.

About a month later, Gary was back, looking around. He wandered around the restaurant with a downcast look. He kept circling the tables and shaking his head.

"What's the problem? Is something else wrong?" Bob asked him.

"Listen," said Gary, beginning to get out his order book, "I don't want to put you to extra expense, but I think those all-white plates make this place look too fancy, not down-home enough. A barbecue place has to have a 'down home' feeling. I have some black-and-white checkered plates that would really make it for you with the red cloths."

This time Bob was a bit more skeptical about the expense. But Gary promised he would take all the plates back on a thirty-day guarantee if Bob would just try them.

Once again Bob placed an order, and once again there was little change in the business. It wasn't that no one was coming in. He had a few steadies, but there just weren't enough people to turn a profit, or even break even. He began to think his family had been right about his business ability.

Two weeks later, Gary buzzed in. "Third time's the charm," he said. I have these new rodeo posters that are all the rage. I can't keep them in stock. Every barbecue place from here to

South Carolina wants them. But I know you're just getting started, and I want you to have the edge. We can put them on the same thirty-day basis as the plates."

Bob was even less certain. But he thought: In for a penny, in for a pound. This was going to be the last thing he tried. He bought the posters.

The thirty days were just about over when Gary reappeared once more. He sat down as if he owned the place, straddling a chair. So, he said, "What's it going to be, cash or returns? It looks like this place is dying. I sure hope you didn't break any of the plates. Bob, you're a nice guy, but the one thing I can't sell you is the taste. If your ribs don't have the taste, no napkins or plates or pictures will make that up."

Bob finally had had it. "What do you mean, I don't have the taste? You never even tasted a single one of my ribs or other dishes. Turn around to the table and sit right." With that, he strode over to Gary and tied a red bib around his neck. Bob unfolded a red napkin with an angry flourish and put the black-and-white checkered plate down so hard that it rattled. He went back to the kitchen and came out with a steaming plate of ribs and chicken.

"Taste this!" Bob demanded.

Gary gingerly picked up a rib and took a small bite, then another and another. He reached for more ribs and finished the chicken too. "This is some good cooking," he said, surprised. "Whose sauce do you use?"

"Whose sauce? Whose sauce do you think? It's mine, made the old-fashioned way."

"Your sauce? Man, you are in the wrong business. Forget the restaurant. Bottle this stuff, and I will sell it from Texas to Florida."

One year later, Bob and Gary celebrated their extraordinary success and the sale of the first million bottles of Bob's Best Barbecue. The party was, of course, in the restaurant. The restaurant still operated on a shoestring. But a million bottles of sauce buys a lot of string.

Career Issues

In the story, Bob asked himself three questions:

- Should I risk my security in order to follow my dream?
- Do I really have the know-how and strength to open a new business?
- What will my family think of me if I fail?

Here are some related career issues that many people face:

- Finding the energy to take a risk in work
- Finding the energy to make a change when feeling burned out
- Finding the energy to take a new path when laid off, "downsized," or fired from work
- Assessing the balance between security and risk

Reflections

This chapter will help you see the sources of energy in your life. It will also help you see that seeming opposites are really two sides of the same coin. So staying still takes as much energy as moving. And risk and security are not opposites. Greater security often comes from taking a risk.

In the first two chapters of the book, you read about change and balance. Energy enables both of these. So whether at this time you are trying to create balance among the roles you play in the parts of your work and life, or you are trying to make a major change in one of those roles, you need energy.

Your own energy is located in the third energy center, which is in the middle of your body, at about the waist. Picture a yellow sun sending its rays throughout your body and you will have a good image of how that chakra can energize every portion of your being. It is no coincidence that we speak of a person who is highly motivated as having "fire in the belly." When we are in touch with that fire, we are each our own energizers.

In our reflections, first we discuss energy in the universe in general. Then we move to the energy within ourselves, and finally we look at how we energize each other. As we look at the swirls of energy within and around Bob, we see how these affect his career, and we explore how you can energize your own career. The sections of these reflections include:

▪ Energy in the Universe

▪ Using Energy in Your Career

▪ Finding the Sources of Energy

Energy in the Universe

In the beginning, all that existed was energy. This concept is supported both by scientific studies and spiritual writings. According to the big bang theory, all matter and energy in the universe come from an explosion that occurred tens of billions of years ago. This began the creation of the cosmos as we experience it today. The creation story in the Book of Genesis says, "In the beginning when God created the heavens and the earth, they were without form and void." This is a description of the absence of matter. We now know from modern physics that everything in the universe is both matter and energy. When energy is in a form, any form, that we humans recognize, we call it *matter* or *mass*.

All mass is made up of atoms. An atom is composed of a center, or nucleus, surrounded by electrons. These electrons can be pictured as a cloud of charge spread out over the entire orbit. When the essence of matter breaks up, the mass is not destroyed. It becomes energy. For example, the splitting of the plutonium atom is called *atomic energy*. But every atom contains energy. Therefore, energy (or its equivalent in mass) can be neither created nor destroyed but it can be changed from one form into another.

The forms of mass and energy can therefore be seen as complements. On the one hand they may appear to be opposites, but on the other hand one does not exist without the other. This principle of complementarity was beautifully expressed by the ancient Chinese poet Lao Tsu (1989), who wrote the *Tao Te Ching*. He talked about a wheel. Picture an old-fashioned wooden wheel with an outer rim, spokes, and an inner rim. The inner rim creates the hole by which the wheel is attached to the wagon. Without the hole, the wheel would have no use. However, what catches our attention is the wheel, not the hole. Lao Tsu also described a clay pitcher or pot. Once again, our attention is caught by the exterior of the pitcher, but that exterior exists only to create the space we fill. The use of the pitcher depends on the space it creates. On the other hand, there is no space without the exterior. What may sound like circular reasoning in the last few sentences is the expression of complementarity. In Lao Tsu's words: "Thirty spokes share the wheel's hub; / It is the center hole that makes it useful. / Shape clay into a vessel; / It is the space within that makes it useful."

Whether we see the exterior of the clay pot as important or we focus on its interior depends on our point of view. If we are looking for a decorative object, we see the exterior. If we want to carry water, our focus is on the utility of the interior. The same duality of the meaning of matter and energy has been discovered in subatomic physics. Picture a piece of metal in which there are

Whether we see the exterior of the clay pot as important or we focus on its interior depends on our point of view. If we are looking for a decorative object, we see the exterior. If we want to carry water, our focus is on the utility of the interior.

two holes. Behind the metal is a recording device. Now, imagine I am able to fire subatomic particles at the recording device behind a wall. The particles divide themselves into waves and behave in the way that waves behave. Just like the waves of the sea, they have what appears to be continuous movement with peaks and valleys. This is true no matter how many particles I fire. Even if I fire only one particle, it divides itself into waves. Now suppose that I have covered one of the holes. The particles I fire now behave like particles, like something with mass. Some of them pass through the hole in the wall, just as a bullet would pass through the hole. Some of them hit the wall and fail to pass through, but none of them becomes waves. Nobody has an explanation for this and no one denies that it's happening.

People think of mass and energy as opposites. However, just as the outside and inside of the pitcher are complements of each other, so particle and wave are complements. In addition, energy is in everything. Sometimes we experience energy as mass and sometimes we experience it as waves; for example, when we hear sounds or look at light. The universe is all energy.

Using Energy in Your Career

The operation of energy in the universe is mirrored in the operation of energy within humans in our careers as well as in all other aspects of our lives. For example, we see decisions as having discrete, separate points, almost as having a mass of their own. We decide to accept a job. That's a separate point. We decide to get married, to buy a house, to sell a car. Each seems to be a separate point. But if we trace the chain of events that led to each decision and that flow from it, we see the operation of waves of thought, experience, and intuition in our lives.

In our story, Bob appeared to be choosing between retirement and starting a new business. That is the view of his decision making as a solid point. However, his process included the peaks of feeling about what he wanted to do, the valleys of fear about losing the capital on which his pension was based, the peaks of the possibilities of providing more for his family, the valleys of self-doubt. That was only one of the waves associated with this story. There were swirls of waves around him. There were the waves of his family's reactions to his plans. There were the waves created by the appearance of the salesman and the salesman's

If we trace the chain of events that led to each decision and that flow from it, we see the operation of waves of thought, experience, and intuition in our lives.

activities. Faced by these waves of energy, we sometimes want to crawl up on a rock. Like a seal or a turtle in rough waters, we seek a safe haven to avoid the power of the energy. Of course we cannot avoid energy, because the very rock beneath us is itself filled with the energy of the universe.

There is an energy in the very tension between growth and safety. Sometimes it is wise to choose growth, to move to an unknown place, like Bob did in opening the restaurant. It is only by taking action that we know what is needed next and can take the next action. Sometimes it is wise to choose safety. If we feel that the energy around us may be overpowering, that we do not have the internal energy to swim in the currents, then we may need to take the time to restore the energy within ourselves.

Earlier we said that the energy in the universe is mirrored in ourselves. The opposite is true as well. The energy within our careers is mirrored in the universe. Sometimes things fall apart. Yeats (1962/1920) began the poem "The Second Coming" with the words: "Things fall apart. The center will not hold." Bob's story is a story of things falling apart. Bob's job fell apart. The restaurant was falling apart. But the very falling apart released the energy necessary for the creation of new structures. When the job fell apart, he was able to create the restaurant. When the restaurant fell apart, he was able to concentrate his energies on the sauce. We can count on this happening in repeated patterns from our knowledge of the universal principle of "dissipative structures." This principle tells us that as structures grow more

As we grow more and more entrenched in work, we are also moving toward the end of that work.

organized, they are moving to dissolution. And as they dissolve, they are moving toward new states of organization. So it is with our careers. As we grow more and more entrenched in work, we are also moving toward the end of that work. And the possibility of new work increases. In fact, we must allow old patterns to dissolve in order to form new, more desirable ones.

This is not simply a matter of changing our job. It is also part of our inner work. How often do we think we have made a big change in our lives—left a job and taken on a new one; left a partner and taken on a new one—only to find that we are reliving the same patterns? Real change does not only come about through actions. Real change comes about through inward sloughing off of patterns of thought so that we may open our eyes to new ways of seeing.

However, whenever disintegration occurs in life, people have choices. Some people emerge better for the change. Others recoup the loss and break even, staying the same. And others spiral downward and despair. Energy is used in all the outcomes, but to create a new set of patterns or a new structure for yourself requires that you consciously marshal your energies and give them direction.

How do we know which direction to take? There is an assumption that the universe always works for us. Those who despair do not buy this assumption. But people who have hope agree with the assumption that the universe is always working for them. When we have hope, our spirits are tuned in to the spirit of the universe. Bob had to be ready to put his energies into the sauce. How he found out about the value of the sauce was through the salesman, his unexpected wise person. He saw this as chance, but was this not the universe working? Let's look at the connection to the energy of the universe as an electric socket. Those who despair are unplugged. Those who simply try to go back to where they were, repeating the same patterns, are only plugged into themselves. People who grow through the change are plugged into the universal energy.

How can you plug into this universal energy? The first step is to recognize that you are part of the universal energy. Remember, all mass and energy are one. Remember that what seem to be opposites are complements. The other side is always there. We have been taught to think logically through all issues. Set aside logic and listen to your intuition. Then look back at the logic too. Allow the logic and the intuition to become one rather

When we have hope, our spirits are tuned in to the spirit of the universe.

than competing forces for your attention. We also tend to listen to the same voices. We may hear the voices of our parents in our heads. We may hear what has been called "the voice of reason." Try listening to voices from unexpected sources. Bob kept "listening" to the salesman until he heard the message he needed to hear—the message about his sauce.

Now, it is true that some of the salesman's ideas seemed to mislead Bob. He spent time and energy going in directions that seemed fruitless. No matter how many plates and napkins he bought, the restaurant was not succeeding. But it was the very utilization of his time and energy in a sustained effort that brought him to the point where he could learn what would bring him the rewards of joy in his work and money. You make the choice as to which voices you heed and as to how long you persevere in any effort.

Sometimes we fear that if we work at something too long, we will lose our energy. It is impossible to lose your energy, until you die. However, it is possible that you will lose interest. Interest is what keeps our energy directed toward a particular effort or work. When we say we feel "burned out," we are using an image of a loss of energy, like an appliance that can no longer get the juice of electricity because its wires are frayed. But humans are not

Feeling burned out is a signal to shift our utilization of energy in a new direction.

toasters. Our wires are our interests, abilities, motivations. Sometimes the feeling comes from a shift in our interest from what we have been doing to some other kind of work. Sometimes the feeling of being burned out or stressed occurs not from a loss of interest, but from having insufficient challenges to our talents or insufficient recognition of those talents by others. And sometimes that burned-out feeling comes from pressures in the organization. Feeling burned out is a signal to shift our utilization of energy in a new direction.

In many ways it is easier to make a change when it is forced on us, when we are "downsized" or otherwise acted upon by outside forces. How often have you thought or heard others say, "I wish they would fire me!" When you begin to wish that the universe would take action to remove you from a situation, it's time to begin to remove yourself. It is harder to make this choice yourself. But the result of not choosing is to remain in a job or work situation that drains the interest that energizes you. You are then faced with Bob's question of assessing security against risk.

Let's use slightly different terms and think of security as safety and risk as growth. Safety is perceived in doing what we have always done, in acting in expected ways. Safety is perceived to exist in sameness. Risk is perceived as taking a different path from the one we expected to take, a path that may have unknown dangers. However, we never truly know what is ahead of us, even on the path that seems most familiar. The many people at all levels of corporations who lost their jobs from the late 1980s to the 1990s thought they were safe in playing the corporate game, in doing the expected. They learned that the safe road also had dangers. So, turn around and see the other side of the picture. Look at the hole, not just the spokes and rim. Look at the purpose of

> *When you begin to wish that the universe would take action to remove you from a situation, it's time to begin to remove yourself.*

your vessel, not just its exterior. Understand that just as there may be risk in safety, there is equally the possibility of security through growth.

One young man we know, Josh, always wanted to go to law school. He prepared himself from middle school through college. He watched law programs on television. He majored in political science because that was a good major for entry into law school. Throughout his senior year in college, he worried about being accepted into law school. When he was accepted into two schools, he was elated. He chose one, began his studies, and did well. However, he just didn't like it. It wasn't what he expected. How could he break away from the direction he had been following for ten years? How could he tell his family he wanted to quit? Would they believe he really wanted to make such a

> *Understand that just as there may be risk in safety, there is equally the possibility of security through growth.*

dramatic shift in direction after only one month? Indeed, when he blurted his feelings out to his family, they thought he didn't know what he was doing. They urged him to complete at least one semester. He stayed for the semester. When he quit, he really didn't know what he wanted to do. So he returned to working in a large retail store where he had worked part time for several summers. He had never paid real attention to the business before. It had just been part of the ticket to law school. Now he saw that this was really what he liked, working with the customers to help them solve their problems. The problems were very different from those that would have come to him as a lawyer, but his effect was more immediate and under his own control. He is now the owner of a successful store.

In Josh's story, we can see the interrelationships of growth and safety. Many would see going to a professional school as growth. But Josh did not feel he was growing there. By leaving the expected path, he grew and later found security as well. He had to give up focus on one path, before he could see the other. Leaving law school enabled him to turn around and see what else was around him. Remember Lao Tsu's poem about the clay vessel, and consider this: If you focus on the outside of the pitcher when you pour, you are likely to make a mess! Josh shifted focus from the clay pot to the space within, from the structure of law school to examination of what he really wanted to do. When Bob kept looking at the ribs, he could not see the sauce.

Finding the Sources of Energy

We have talked about the universality of energy and how energy is in all matter. However, in our ordinary human lives, we talk about and feel the necessity to find ways to "energize" ourselves. What are some of the sources of energy? When we feel it's the time in our careers to make a change or to figure out a change to make, what can we draw upon to give us that sense of an energy boost? We know from personal experience and observing others that the same energizers do not work for all people. Some of us are Duracell folks, others are Eveready, and still others prefer a generic battery.

A major difference has been found between people who are energized by being with others and those who are energized by being alone. Think of what you do after a tiring day. One person we know picks up the telephone to call friends whenever she returns home tired from her work. This is despite the fact that her work brings her in contact with many people during the day.

This is a person who is energized by strong interpersonal relationships. Another person, in a similar situation, comes home, picks up the daily newspaper, and prefers to unwind quietly in a room by herself.

However, both of these people can be energized by people who are themselves sparking with energy. There is a story about people who are each sparks of the one universal fire: It is only when the sparks come together—into contact with each other—that they become a flame.

We connect with each other not only through direct or electronic contact, but through other expressions of our creations. For this reason, we are energized by music, painting and other visual arts, live theater and motion pictures, and books. This is true whether we are participating ourselves in the creative process or enjoying the creations of others.

Physical activity is another source of energy. From sandlot baseball games and schoolyard pick-up basketball to aerobic exercise in the newest fitness center, we gain energy by expending energy. And anyone who doubts the energy enrichment of spectator sports need look no further than watching a group of people at a basketball game.

Just as physical activity gives us energy, so does the quiet of being alone. Sometimes we need to be alone to gather the energy of our thoughts. Sometimes it is important simply to sit in a state of awareness of our own bodies, our breathing, and the sounds inside and outside ourselves. Many would call this meditation, and some of the exercises in this book draw on the energizing effects of meditation. Meditation has been found most effective when it is practiced daily. Many religious traditions celebrate a day of rest every seven days. The day of rest usually includes some communal prayer and some time alone. Ritualizing rest and aloneness may provide more energy than occasional, unscheduled attempts at solitude.

Possibly the most empowering source of energy for work is the work itself. When your work is work you love, it generates its own energy. This energizing nature of doing work that you love and about which you care deeply has been called *flow*. Flow is the awareness that you are doing what you are doing for its own sake, you are doing it to the best of your ability, and you enjoy what you are doing.

You will need to identify for yourself the ways you have of finding energy, of recharging your batteries. Then instead of bringing the stresses of the job home to your family, you can

Possibly the most empowering source of energy for work is the work itself. When your work is work you love, it generates its own energy.

bring the energy you get from work and activities outside of work back to the job itself and home to your family. Thus you are participating in the unending pool of universal energy.

Energy and Spirituality—
Some Concluding Thoughts

This chapter is about understanding energy so that we can use it to take risks and make necessary changes. In *Modern Man in Search of a Soul*, Carl Jung (1933/1931) wrote about the dilemma that many of his clients faced. He described them as well-adapted individuals who were nevertheless dissatisfied with their lives, who felt a sense of emptiness. He used the phrase "I am stuck" to describe their feelings. In simplest terms, this chapter is about getting unstuck.

Applications

In this chapter we looked at the need to find and use energy in our work so that we can face the challenges of risk and change. The applications that follow are designed to help you in four ways:

∎ To identify the sources of energy in your life

∎ To assess the balance between risk and security

∎ To identify what you must let go of to go forward

∎ To identify what you have missed by focusing too intently on the obvious or familiar

Application 1: Me in the Middle

Remember we talked about being stuck between growth and safety. This is an exercise to help you get unstuck. The exercise helps you look at where you are now, figure out where you want to go, and then identify sources of energy in your life as well as barriers to growth or change. Finally, it helps you look at overcoming those barriers through further use of your energy.

Directions: Acquire a box of crayons and a piece of paper, at least 8½″ by 11″. Copy the diagram on page 79 onto the larger sheet of paper, holding the paper horizontally.

In the box on the left, draw a picture of your career as you see it now. Include all elements that you believe are important, such as relationships with others, the work you do, the relationship between your work and your family, the physical environment in which you work, the relationship between your work and your spirituality.

Select a date in the future by which you would like to have made changes in your career. In the box on the right, draw a picture of your career as you would like it to be on that date.

Choose a coin, crayon, or token of some sort to represent you, and place it in the middle box halfway between the present and the future. Identify the factors in your life that will get you to the future you have pictured. Write them to the left of your token in the middle box with an arrow pointing to the future. Be sure to consider both external and internal factors. Now identify the external and internal factors in your life that may keep you from that pictured future. Write them on the right-hand side of your token with an arrow pointing to the past.

Think about how you can add power to the forces moving you to the future. Add some key words or phrases to the left of your token. Move your token closer to the future.

Look again at the challenges to your future. Identify the energies that can help you overcome these challenges. Describe the energies in key words or phrases in the left-hand column, and again move your token to the future.

See if you can move your token to the future one more time by identifying still more sources of energy and support to help you change.

Then complete the worksheet "Me in the Middle: Getting Unstuck" with the information you have learned about yourself in this exercise.

Me in the Middle

My Career Today	Forces: Energies vs. challenges	My Career in _____ (date)
	Me	

Me in the Middle: Getting Unstuck

This is how I plan to change my life:

This is the energy I bring to the change—internal energy:

This is the energy I bring to the change—external energy:

These are the internal hurdles I must still overcome:

These are the external hurdles I must still overcome:

This is the energy I will use to overcome these hurdles:

Application 2: The Magic Mirror of Complementarity

This application will help you see what you have missed by focusing too intently on the obvious or the familiar.

Directions: Imagine that you have a mirror with a magic button. When you look in the mirror, holding it up in front of your face, you see your face. But when you press the button, you see right through your face and head, as if they were transparent, to all that is behind your head.

Now focus the mirror on your situation at work. You can see all the patterns of behavior and thought you see every day. You can see all the problems and all the solutions you have rejected. Now press the magic button. What can you see that you could not see before? Record your ideas in the spaces provided.

What I see without my mirror	What I see through the magic mirror

Application 3: A Meditation on Energy

Directions: You may want to ask someone else to read this slowly to you, or you may want to read the meditation into a tape recorder for yourself before you begin. This meditation begins like all the others with directions that will put you in a receptive frame of mind and spirit.

Sit in a comfortable chair with a firm back, or on the floor with your back straight and your legs crossed comfortably. Place your hands on your thighs, palms up and slightly open. Straighten yourself as if you were about to pay attention. Now let your shoulders drop naturally. Breathe slowly in through your nose and out through your mouth. You may make a sound with your breath as you exhale. That's fine. Just breathe in and out deeply and evenly for a few moments. Let your breath return to normal.

Begin to feel the power of the earth wherever your body is in contact with the floor or chair. Maintain your contact with the abundant power of the physical, material world. Let the energy of the brown and red earth, its dryness, its moist fertility enter your body. Keep the earth's energy within you. At the same time, become aware of the top of your head. Imagine you can feel the electricity of all the spirit in the cosmos. As you draw in one breath, draw in the abundance of the earth. Exhale. As you draw in the next breath, draw in the light of the cosmos. Picture this as you breathe in and out. Any time you lose your concentration in the exercise, just return to your breathing.

Turn your attention to the base of your spine, the first energy center. Picture a red disk spinning round and round. As you breathe, feel the energy of your breath moving the disk. As the red disk moves, feel it energizing your breath. Now move your attention to your pelvic area and picture an orange disk spinning. Breathe in and out of the orange disk.

Move your attention to the area of your waist. The third energy center is a yellow disk at the center of your body. Open the yellow center by breathing into its spinning. Feel the spinning make your very breath yellow. Picture it as being as bright as healing sunshine. This is your source of health and energy.

If you have any spots in your body that do not feel well, use your breath to move the healing yellow energy to those spots. Take a few moments for healing breaths of yellow energy. Feel the sunshine in your body.

Now picture yourself at your place of work or your ideal place of work. Be specific in what you see. See yourself in the office, classroom, store, or factory, wherever you work. Let yourself see your workplace in full living color and motion. Bring the yellow energy of your belly to your workplace. Bring it to all the parts of yourself that you use at work, to your mind, to your hands, to your voice, to your legs and feet. Feel the yellow energy flowing through your body parts into the work so that you are one with what you are doing. Feel the ball of yellow energy expanding within and beyond the boundaries of your body so that all you are doing is surrounded by health and energy. Breathe in and out of that large ball of energy. Now breathe in and out letting the ball of energy return to the center of your body.

Keeping your eyes closed and your breath normal, repeat the following affirmations four times aloud or silently:

I am able to see the future I want.
I have the energy to create the future I want.

When you are ready, slowly open your eyes.

Application 4: In Your Own Voice— Continuing Your Journal

Continue your journal by noting your thoughts on the story of Bob. Consider the reflections that followed the story. Did they raise any questions or ideas for your own use? You may also want to include ideas that came to you when you did the other applications for this chapter. Think about what energy means in your own life.

Think about the following questions. Answer them right away but also continue to let the questions float around your mind so that you can add more information as it comes to you. What are sources of energy in your life? Where are you in the balance between risk and security in your current job? If you want to go forward, what must you give up?

Community

Beatrice at the Beginning

The Story

"Dr. Stevens, do you have to leave? I don't see how I will get through my comps without you."

"Your comps? How am I going to get through my life without you, Prof. Stevens?"

"Professor, please, just before you go, look at my electives list just one more time and tell me whether to take the Dante or the Cervantes seminar."

Beatrice Stevens looked at the group of juniors sitting around her South Atlantic University office. She knew she would really miss these kids, her babies as she called them in her head—but never to them. Beatrice had been a professor for twenty-five years, all at South Atlantic. She had come to SAU as a newly minted Ph.D. as soon as she had finished her studies in romance languages at the Sorbonne.

As the last students drifted out of her office with their final chorus of reluctant farewells, Beatrice looked around at the home she was planning to leave. The files still had the last dusty pile of journal article clippings, the ones she had decided not to use in her latest book. The four books themselves were lined up on the first shelf of the bookcase. She felt gratified by the letters she had received from colleagues who told her how helpful they had found her work on language teaching. She leaned back in her chair remembering all the satisfying moments in her career, and then, some of the less happy times crept into her thoughts.

She recalled the thick folder on the linguistic devices of Renaissance Italian poets. That was to have been her first book, a book she never wrote. Initially, when she returned to the United States from the Sorbonne, she had been so happy to get a university position. She saw herself in a life of scholarly contemplation. But that's not how things developed. From the first years on, she had been tapped to work with students, then with new colleagues. Freshman orientation to freshman orientation, she called it to herself. How ironic. Her first career choice, nursing, had been working with people. She thought as a young woman that she had given people up for books, but she had ended up working with people after all.

Beatrice shook herself out of her chair. She had not "ended up" anywhere. This was not the end but the beginning of the next part of her career. Now, with the financial security of retirement, she was going back to her first love. While she was not actually going to become a trained nurse, she had signed up as a virtually full-time volunteer at the Howard Hospice. She looked in the mirror, gave her short graying curls a shake, and put on lipstick. It was time for her SAU retirement party.

Beatrice walked across the campus to the faculty club. The warm evening air felt good against her face. As she drew closer to the faculty club, she straightened her shoulders. She knew faculty. Many there would be happy for her. Others would be envious. Some would remember past campus battles and have their guard up—or their weapons out. All of them would have strong opinions and none would be shy about expressing them.

Beatrice walked into the club and heard the noise of the party. It was already underway. As she entered the room, people turned, applauded, and lifted their glasses in salute.

"Beatrice, you look wonderful. But you always do. Are you going to take any kind of a break between working here and going to the hospital?"

"Hospice, not hospital," Beatrice explained for what seemed like the hundredth time.

"What's the difference?" chimed in another guest. Aren't both of them for sick people?"

"A hospital is a place where they try to make you well, to keep you alive," answered Beatrice. "A hospice is a place where you go to die. The purpose is to make dying as comfortable, as peaceful, as possible." For a moment, her thoughts flashed on the last days of her mother's life, an image of needles and tubes that never left her for long.

"Well, I just don't know why you are doing this. I guess you want to make some sort of 'contribution,' but you do that right here. If you want to work, why not stay on? You know your pension will continue to grow."

"Not to mention," another colleague added, "we really need you here. Your work on the committee to improve college teaching has really just begun."

"And your students are crazy about you."

"Remember, that hospital—okay, hospice—isn't paying you a penny. Don't you think that there would be pay for the work if it were really worthwhile? That's how we measure worth in our good, capitalistic society. Money shows your worth."

"Why not work on your books?"

"How's about just good old 'R and R'?"

"You know, with your language ability and the global economy, you could probably make a fortune consulting."

Dean Robertson broke into the chorus of questioners. "Give her a break, folks. This is supposed to be a celebration. Let's take our guest of honor to the front of the room where we can honor her properly."

Beatrice was glad when the ceremonies and celebration ended. She knew that even her closest friends did not understand her desire to work in a hospice. But Beatrice herself knew exactly what she wanted. Her mother's slow and painful death, when Beatrice was only eighteen, had almost directed her into a career in nursing. She had not gone that route because she already was committed to a scholarship in languages. But she did want to make a difference to people. She wanted to help people live their lives—and end them—with dignity and calm. She had worked on the first part for the past twenty-five years. Now she was going to work on the second.

That was Friday. The weekend passed, and on Monday Beatrice reported to work at the Howard Hospice. As had been explained to her when she signed up, the first week was devoted to training. She recognized that it was important to learn the hospice routines. And it was certainly helpful to know where the supplies were kept and when to call a doctor or trained nurse. But time and again Bea found herself annoyed with the teaching itself. Her thoughts wandered from the material she was learning to how she believed the training should be presented. Each night, Bea lectured herself on her new role, on relinquishing her status as a teacher. It certainly felt strange to be a student once more.

In the second and following weeks, Bea plunged into the work of the hospice. It wasn't easy. She had pictured herself soothing foreheads, holding hands, reading quiet works, and listening to people's worries. She did these things some of the time, but not most of the time. Most of the time, she was helping the professional staff with the physical care of patients. At those times, she felt that she was the most educated bedpan dumper in the world. What had happened to Dr. Stevens, Prof. Stevens? Who was she? Few patients even knew her first name, let alone who she really was. Or was it who she really had been?

Night after night she went home exhausted. Sometimes it was morning before she went home. Volunteers are needed around the clock. When she was most tired, she heard the voices of the naysayers at her party and began to ask herself, have I done the right thing? What do I need this for? Beatrice decided to give the hospice work a three-month trial. She had signed up for that amount of time and was not a quitter.

On Wednesday of the last week of the third month, Beatrice got herself ready for one more day, thinking only two more to go.

Arriving at the hospice, she looked at the roster of assignments on the bulletin board. Great, she thought, I've been assigned to stay with Joseph. He was a very angry man who had not accepted his dying. None of the hospice regimen that makes dying easier for most people had worked for him. He seemed to hold the hospice responsible for his pain and condition. As Beatrice entered the room, she realized that the first thing she would have to do was to change his sheets.

But even before she could begin to get things ready, Joseph started in on her. "What's wrong with you? Are you stupid? How can you let me lie here like this? Why do they hire dummies like you? It's inhuman. I hate you."

"It's inhuman" reverberated throughout Beatrice's being. She remembered her mother and how inhuman she had found the hospital. She knew that she was no "dummy." The hospice was indeed a more humane place for dying than the hospital. Her job was to ease Joseph's dying, not to get him to love her. She had to be there for all of the Josephs. They were not there for her.

Career Issues

In this story, Beatrice faced four questions related to her early retirement from a job in which she had invested many years of energy and interest:

▪ What contribution can I make to improve the lives of others?

▪ How will I make it in this new setting in which I don't know the people or the job?

▪ How do others see me now that I no longer have the position I had?

▪ Who am I now that I no longer have the title I had?

Here are some related career issues that many people face:

▪ Relating who we are and what we want to do to needs of the community

▪ Dealing with changes in work communities as a result of retirement or other career moves

▪ Establishing our identity in a new community

▪ Finding our identity beyond our occupational title

Reflections

The story of Beatrice is the story of an ongoing search for community. Beatrice may seem like an extreme example to most of us. First she dedicated her entire professional career to providing service to students. Then she sought to give even more service through full-time volunteer work. However, each of us has a parallel desire for connections with others. We have this desire because we instinctively know that we find ourselves through loving, caring, and reaching out to other people. We can call this a *sense of community.*

The sense of community is expressed through the energy center of the body located near the heart. Picture your heart

We know that we want to give and receive love, but we are often confused about how we can satisfy our desire for community in the rush of today's world.

beating into a megaphone. The narrow end of the megaphone is at your heart. The wide end of the megaphone is as wide as you want to make it. Through the megaphone you send your love into the world. However, the wide end of the megaphone also brings back love, funneling it into your heart. In "Renascence," the poet Edna St. Vincent Millay (1917) wrote, "The world stands out on either side no wider than the heart is wide." Through the megaphone of love we widen our hearts.

We know that we want to give and receive love, but we are often confused about how we can satisfy our desire for community in the rush of today's world. In these reflections, we will look at several ideas about our relationship to community. The first idea is that meaning in life comes from our connection to others. Second, we will look at the varied kinds of communities in which we live and work. The third part of these reflections is about how we relate to community as individuals. In the concluding thoughts to these reflections, we link the concepts of meaning, community, and spirituality. The sections of the reflections are as follows:

- Finding Meaning Through Connections to Others
- Varied Communities — Many Opportunities for Participation
- Kinds of Connections

Finding Meaning Through Connections to Others

Living with a sense of connection to others is the same as living in community, and this is the same as living in love. You may wonder how this is related to your career. Wonder no longer. "Work is love made visible," wrote Kahlil Gibran in *The Prophet* (1951).

As human beings, we have an innate drive to live and work with one another. The infant human cannot survive without the community of at least one adult. As we mature, our community only grows larger. We enlarge our view from the community of child and mother to the community of the larger family. We

As human beings, we have an innate drive to live and work with one another.

begin to learn the community of the neighborhood and the school, in whatever form it takes. Finally, as adults, we experience the larger world in which we live.

In the story, Beatrice began to experience the world in a heartfelt way when she saw how her mother died. This influenced her to want to help other people. She thought she could do this through scholarly writing, so she became a professor. However, over and over again she chose more direct forms of helping others. She helped students and assisted new teachers. She became known in the community of her university as someone people could count on. But Beatrice's memory of her mother's slow and painful death remained with her throughout her life, and this memory led her back to her original desire to alleviate the suffering of the dying.

Beatrice's love for others and service to others did not necessarily make her seem lovable in the usual sense. Other faculty members took verbal swipes at her at the retirement party. Joseph railed at her from his sickbed. Beatrice's connection with community was not founded on getting love, but on giving it.

The perennially popular author Stephen Covey writes as one of his *Seven Habits of Highly Effective People* (1989), "Seek not to be understood, but to understand." This is a modern restatement of part of the prayer of Saint Francis (1952): "O divine master, grant that I may not so much seek . . . to be understood as to understand." In other words, in order to find meaning in our own lives, in our own work, in whatever we do, we must reach out to others and understand them. It is only through understanding others that we begin to understand our own meaning and purpose in life. If you remember the complementarity principle discussed in the previous chapter, you may see this as one more example of the flipping coin.

Not everybody finds meaning in work that can be identified

It is only through understanding others that we begin to understand our own meaning and purpose in life.

as direct service to others. Hospice work is not for everybody, neither is being a professor. But participation in community is essential for all people who seek meaningful lives. The key to finding meaning lies in the recognition of the many communities in which we participate and in the conscious evaluation of the quality of our participation.

The quality of our participation in community offers joy in life. We dance with others. We sing with others. And we laugh along with others in the darkness of a movie theater. Even people who seem to be alone in prayer are really members of praying communities. Some religious groups may isolate themselves physically from the larger world, but they do so to affect that world through prayer.

On the other hand, some people cannot see their attachment to any people. They experience neither community nor communality. Like Edgar Allen Poe's (1985/1840) "Man in the Crowd," they move around the periphery of society, mistaking crowds for company or community. In the story, a man goes from bar to bar until all the bars close. Eventually he disappears into the night alone. Although these unattached people are in the presence of others, they feel and act as if they were alone in the world. In *The Lonely Crowd*, David Riesman (1950), a sociologist, extended Poe's image. Riesman, writing from the vantage point of the 1950s, suggested that our society itself produces separation of one person from another while trying for community through conformity.

Poe suggested in the story that this disconnected man has the characteristics of the quintessential criminal because he has no sense of community. Indeed, it is not a great leap to believe that one cannot commit crimes against others if one understands our essential interdependence. "Justice begins with the recognition of the necessity of sharing," wrote philosopher Elias Canetti in *Crowds and Power* (1984/1960). This concept of the importance

It is the interdependent nature of human beings that we express when we work in authentic relationships with others.

of community in combating many of American society's ills is the basis of the Communitarian Network. This movement is under the leadership of Amitai Etzioni (1994), who is not only a highly regarded scholar but also an adviser to presidents and an activist. And, of course, being an activist is itself participation in community.

Community, we have seen, brings meaning to each of our lives, and our individual participation in community through connections to others brings meaning to their lives. It is the interdependent nature of human beings that we express when we work in authentic relationships with others. Seeking authentic relationships with others is the opposite of finding people to meet one's needs. As Krishnamurti wrote in *On Right Livelihood* (1992/1958), "When we use work or people as a means to an end, then obviously we have no relationship, no communion either with the work or with people, and then we are incapable of love. Love is not a means to an end; it is its own eternity."

Varied Communities— Many Opportunities for Participation

As adults we have some choice about the communities in which we wish to participate. While we are born into our families, we can choose to be active or inactive family members. We can even choose to remove ourselves from all contact with relatives, but the family membership does not disappear. It continues to influence our experiences and decisions. Also, we were born in a particular geographic location and raised in a particular culture, which includes religion. We may choose to move. We may choose to educate ourselves in the ways of one or more other cultures. We may choose to change our religion or practice no religion. Although we remain influenced by where we have been, we can choose where we are going.

In the story, Beatrice illustrates one kind of community change we all may face through choice or circumstance— a change in our work community. Beatrice was an active member of the university community. When she left her job, she relinquished her active status in that community. She may retain a

Although we remain influenced by where we have been, we can choose where we are going.

place in the community of friends she has formed from the university, but her new active work community is the hospice. In this new community she must establish new relationships. She has to reveal her identity to people who have not known her before.

How can we establish ourselves in a new community? The first step is listening. What do we learn from the people who are already there? In the story, Beatrice literally becomes a student again. Not all new work situations offer orientation programs. And even when they do, you will not learn all you need to know from the official program. Remember: "Seek first to understand and then to be understood." This is the learning or induction stage. After you have completed your learning or induction, you enter into a transition stage. In the transition stage, you make judgments about your relationship to the community. You need to ask yourself: Do I really fit into this new community? How do I fit? You do this by acting, speaking, being yourself in the community. This is a test. It's not a test of you nor of the community, but a test of the goodness of fit between you and the community. If the fit is good, you then maintain yourself in the community by continuing to participate in its purpose.

When one community is not satisfying, we look to other communities for satisfaction of our need for interrelatedness and the meaning that comes from it.

What does "participate in the purpose of a community" mean in relation to your job? It means carrying out the work for which you are responsible to the best of your ability. It also means seeing your work as a part of the interlocking functions of all work in that organization. Then your definition of your job is not shallow, but incorporates a depth of understanding of the mutual relationships that produce success for the organization. When each person understands the mutual relationships, a community exists.

The workplace, however, is not the only source of satisfying community relationships. Indeed, despite our best efforts, some work organizations are more "lonely crowds" than communities. When one community is not satisfying, we look to other communities for satisfaction of our need for interrelatedness and the meaning that comes from it. However, it is not only when we are dissatisfied that we look for other sources of connectedness.

It is often when we are feeling most satisfied that we can spread our love in other groups. We can look at other communities as falling into three categories: the communities of companionship, the communities of culture, and the cosmic community.

The communities of companionship include family units and close friendships. A natural community is created by the family in which we live. Whether we live in traditional two-parent, extended families; single-parent families; or families of unrelated adults living together; or how geographically close we are to members of our families, what is really at issue is the nature of our relationships. When we step into the shoes of others, experience empathy, understand where someone else is coming from, we build community. This is parallel to the formal induction into a work organization. Understanding must precede any idea that we can help someone else or be of service to them in a meaningful way.

There are many communities of culture in which you can participate. They include the neighborhood in which you live, groups formed around leisure or professional interests, and religious organizations. There is a neighborhood culture, a way of

When we step into the shoes of others, experience empathy, understand where someone else is coming from, we build community.

doing things and believing how things should be done that is unique to different towns or parts of cities. This is true whether you live in a small town or large city. We have the image that small towns provide a greater sense of community than large, crowded cities. This is not always true. Small towns can be havens for individuals living in isolation, and neighborhoods in large cities often provoke vibrant participation. As in all the other examples, community is formed from my sense of my interrelatedness with you, your sense of interrelatedness with me, and the actions that flow from that mutual sense.

You may find satisfaction through communities formed around leisure or professional interests. While some people may think that leisure activities and work are incompatible, you can do valuable work in leisure. This includes not only the obvious help you can provide others through charitable activities, but work that contributes to the beauty of the world and to fun for yourself and others. Finding any work that needs doing connects your work to the work of the universe.

Cosmic communities are movements around big ideas, often sparked by the influence of charismatic leaders. Mother Teresa went off alone to serve the dying poor, and a community

Whatever we do to bring peace among people or improve the environment brings us into interrelatedness with others.

formed around her. When Princess Diana died, a grieving community emerged. Many Americans who remember the death of John F. Kennedy in 1963 are members of a community who share the memories of where they were when they learned of his death. They were interrelated in their grief and remain so in their memories. Rosa Parks, Ben and Jerry, Mahatma Gandhi, and Golda Meir are all examples of leaders around whom communities formed. In our own communities, we often see the emergence of the informal leader, the one people turn to when office politics become hot or other issues emerge. You have probably been involved in such a community. You may participate in the work of the universe by uniting behind those leaders or movements that incorporate your values. Indeed, you may become one of the leaders yourself.

The ultimate cosmic community is the world community. Whatever we do to bring peace among people or improve the environment brings us into interrelatedness with others. This connection of people to the land was expressed in the following quotation attributed to Chief Seattle (1991/1855). When he sold land to the United States government, he said, "Every part of this earth is sacred to my people. Every shining pine needle, every sandy shore, every mist in the dark woods, every meadow are holy in the memory of my people. . . . We are brothers to the beasts . . . sisters to the flowers."

Kinds of Connections

Just as there are varied communities in which you can participate, so are there different ways to connect. Indeed, we know that some people derive energy from being with others, while others gain energy from being alone. Carl Jung, in *Modern Man in Search of a Soul* (1933/1931), called these personality preferences *extroversion* and *introversion*.

Regardless of your personality preference, you can make connections. Some people, the extroverts, relate to communities in an active, social manner. Others, the introverts, relate to people more passively, taking in information and acting on it only when they are certain of what they want to do. These people can be perceived as less social and yet their contributions are equally valuable. They just do it in a different way. For example, the extrovert, seeing a need for stoplights at a school intersection, may organize a group to rally at a city council meeting. The introvert, seeing the same problem, may gather facts and write a letter to the newspaper. Both are participating in community in a way that is comfortable for their personality preferences. Even the writer or artist who squirrels work away in an attic is making connections. Think of Emily Dickinson or J. D. Salinger.

We can look at ways to connect from another perspective. William Schutz (1978) developed a theory of interpersonal needs. He described three needs for connectedness: the need for inclusion, the need for control, and the need for affection. For each need, a person may prefer to be the actor, including others, taking control, expressing affection. Or a person may prefer to be the recipient, being included by another, acting within a structure set by another, or receiving affection from another. It is most important to know that none of the needs is in itself a good or a bad thing. It is equally important to know that it is not preferable to be the actor or the recipient. In fact, some people have no strong preference for either role. They can be happy as the actor or the recipient depending upon the situation. For you to be successful in your relationships and happy in your community, you do need to know your own interpersonal needs, your own likes and dislikes.

When you think of the *need for inclusion*, think of recognition, attention, participation, contact, and belonging. If you are the actor, you like to include others in your life. You may prefer activities like speaking before groups, forming new groups, giving parties, telling jokes, or organizing meetings. If you are the recipient, you like to be included in groups by others and get recognition from them. You would probably prefer activities like going to the water cooler where you will meet other people, taking an active part in group discussions, joining already formed groups, and joining others in decorating the workplace or community center. Although you probably have a consistent style of behaving, that is, you generally prefer to be an actor or a recipient, circumstance may influence your preference. Furthermore, circumstance can also influence how strongly you feel the need for inclusion.

When you think of the *need for control*, think of power, authority, influence, and management. If you are the actor, you prefer to influence or direct others. You probably like working in an environment where you are trusted to do tasks with minimum supervision; you enjoy positions of leadership; you like to establish policies and set the structure for others; you enjoy competition. If you are the recipient, you like to get help and precise instructions. You prefer being in an unpressured environment. You may enjoy the planning stages of projects. You value free time. Remember, your style of operation and strength of need may be influenced by circumstance.

The *need for affection* involves empathy, affirmation, support, warmth, and faithfulness. If you prefer to be the actor, you like to be warm, reassuring, intimate, and concerned. You feel comfortable in situations that have a high degree of intimacy and in which you may talk about what's important to you. You like to be able to show your appreciation for other people. If you prefer to be the recipient, you like to feel the support of others, but you don't often show your own feelings of warmth. You may have difficulty saying "no" to requests for help. Once again, the interpersonal needs that motivate us may be modified by particular circumstances.

Finally, what we connect with and how we connect will relate not only to our interpersonal needs and personality preferences, but also to what we value. We may value productivity, beauty, service to others. Each of these and any combination of these are valid sources of connections and community. Through the expression of our values in our community, we reveal to ourselves and others who we are and who we want to become. In our story, Joseph, the dying patient, was the wise person for Beatrice. He helped her see that her sense of community was derived from

> *Through the expression of our values in our community, we reveal to ourselves and others who we are and who we want to become.*

her interpersonal needs for affection and inclusion as well as the value that she placed on service. She had the same needs and values in the hospice community as she had had in the college community. Joseph enabled her to see how they were now going to be lived out.

Meaning, Community, and Spirituality— Some Concluding Thoughts

Spirituality encompasses the awareness of oneness with others in the here and now so that the sense of self is subsumed in sense of community. There is a story by O'Henry (1905), "The Gift of the Magi," that is known to many people. This is the story of a community of two, a marriage. It is Christmas. The couple have no money for gifts. The husband, knowing how his wife prides herself on her beautiful hair, sells his beloved pocket watch to buy her a comb. The wife, knowing how much her husband cherishes his watch, sells her hair to buy him a watch chain. They think only of each other and sacrifice their most precious material possessions. What they gain is a sense of the love that binds them as a community and that unites them to universal love.

Just as the two people in the O'Henry story forget themselves in their concern for the other, so may we do this in larger communities. When the individual's desires are for the welfare of the group, even the conception of work changes. Rather than seeing work solely as a means to make a living or to establish one's status, work is also seen as part of the great enterprise of creation. Each individual is then a participant in the co-creation of all that is good.

Sometimes we think we gain most when we act for the self alone. In the O'Henry story, might the couple have been better off if they had not sold or bought anything? He would have his watch, she would have her hair. But they would have had less of each. It is difficult to conceptualize the benefit to be gained from putting community ahead of self in societies where individualism has a strong hold. It's important to remember that other cultures put the group ahead of the individual. For example, we see our very dreams as expressions of our individual psyches, and tend to believe that all people do so. However, traveling in Australia, the psychologist Robert Bosnak (1996) learned that the aboriginal people interpret their dreams only in terms of meaning for the group. This is perfectly consistent with their cultural preference for a collective, rather than an individualistic, society.

As Danah Zohar and Ian Marshall point out in *The Quantum Society* (1995), we may all be part of a collective whether that is our choice or not. In the chapter on energy, we described the complementary nature of particles and waves. Zohar and Marshall suggest that each individual operates as a particle, a point in the here and now. But collectively (all the points) we are waves, interacting and reconstructing ourselves through these interactions. So we are both individuals and community.

This concept of the power of the one in the many has permeated the world's religions throughout time. In Judaism, there is a requirement that ten people gather together each morning and evening to pray. In Christianity, there is the same idea. Jesus said, "Wherever two or three are gathered in my name, there I am in the midst of them." In the settlements of modern-day Pueblo Indians as well as in the ancient sites of the Anasazi, we see kivas, underground ceremonial chambers where people gathered in community for sacred rites. Pilgrimages by Moslems to the Kaaba, the central shrine in Mecca, is still one more example of the power of community in the spiritual life.

Participation in organized religion is not the only path to spirituality in community. D. H. Lawrence (1977/1924) wrote, "Men are free when they belong to a living, organic, *believing* community, active in fulfilling some unfulfilled, perhaps unrealized purpose. . . . Men are not free when they are doing just what they like. The moment you can do just what you like, there is nothing you care about doing." The spiritual key is in the belonging itself.

Applications

In this chapter we examined the importance of community in your work, in your personal and social activities, and in your spiritual connections. The applications that follow are designed to help you in your career in three ways:

▪ To identify the strategies you use to face the challenge of job change

▪ To identify the communities in which you now participate

▪ To assess your involvement and satisfaction in those communities

Application 1: Goodness of Fit Questionnaire

This is an exercise to use when you are changing jobs. It will help you identify strategies to use to check out the organization and how good the fit is between you and the organization. In other words, these are strategies for the induction and transition stages of a new job. Of course, you may also adapt the questions to examine how you fit into any new community.

Directions: Complete the sentences below. It may take some time on a new job, or other new situation, to be able to answer all the questions in both the induction and transition parts. When you have finished answering all the questions, you should have a pretty good idea of how well you and the organization in which you work fit together.

Goodness of Fit Questionnaire

A. The Induction

1. When I first came to this job, I gained information by reading the organization literature about:

2. When I first came to this job, I gained information by listening to formal statements about:

3. When I first came to this job, I gained information by listening to my boss talk about:

4. When I first came to this job, I gained information by listening to my co-workers talk about:

5. When I first came to this job, I gained information when people asked me about:

6. I have learned all I need to know about:

7. I would like to learn more about:

8. I can get that information by:

B. The Transition

1. When I think about what I've learned, I feel:

2. When I speak or make suggestions, people in this organization tend to:

3. When I take action at work, people in the organization tend to:

---

4. My values and the values of the people around me are:

5. My values and the values of the organization as a whole are:

6. When I think about all that has happened so far, I think my future in the organization is:

Application 2: Circles of Participation

This application is designed to help you assess how your interpersonal needs for inclusion, control, and attachment are satisfied through the communities in which you participate.

Directions: These four circles represent the major types of communities discussed in the reflections: work, companionship, culture, and the cosmic community. Each circle is divided into three parts. Each part stands for an interpersonal need: inclusion, control, or affection.

For each community type, identify a specific community in which you participate. For example, in the work circle, you might think of your whole organization or a project team within it. In the culture circle, you might identify a club or a professional group. Then in each portion of the circle, list the actions you commonly take within that community. When you have finished, consider any changes in activities you would like to make.

Circles of Participation

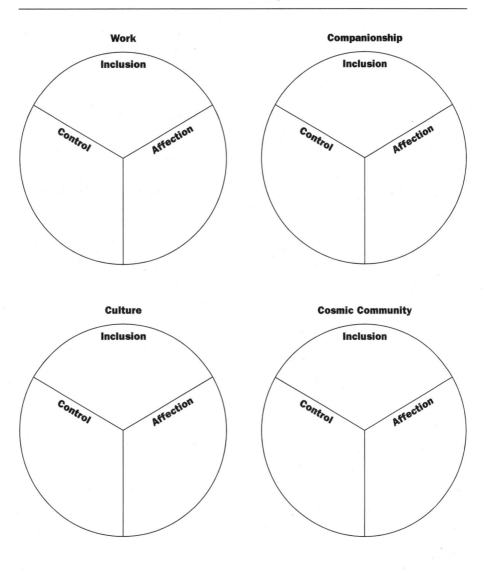

Application 3: A Meditation on Community

Directions: You may want to ask someone else to read this slowly to you, or you may want to read the meditation into a tape recorder for yourself before you begin. This meditation begins like all the others with directions that will put you in a receptive frame of mind and spirit.

Sit in a comfortable chair with a firm back, or on the floor with your back straight and your legs crossed comfortably. Place your hands on your thighs, palms up and slightly open. Straighten yourself as if you were about to pay attention. Now let your shoulders drop naturally. Breathe slowly in through your nose and out through your mouth. You may make a sound with your breath as you exhale. That's fine. Just breathe in and out deeply and evenly for a few moments. Let your breath return to normal.

Begin to feel the power of the earth wherever your body is in contact with the floor or chair. Maintain your contact with the abundant power of the physical, material world. Let the energy of the brown and red earth, its dryness, its moist fertility enter your body. Keep the earth's energy within you. At the same time, become aware of the top of your head. Imagine you can feel the electricity of all the spirit in the cosmos. As you draw in one breath, draw in the abundance of the earth. Exhale. As you draw in the next breath, draw in the light of the cosmos. Picture this as you breathe in and out. Any time you lose your concentration in the exercise, just return to your breathing.

Move your attention to the first energy center, the one at the base of your spine. See the red disk spinning at that energy center. Breathe in and out of the red disk several times.

Now move your attention to your pelvis. Picture an orange disk spinning around your pelvis. This is the energy of your second energy center. Breathe into the orange disk.

Move your attention to the third energy center at your midsection. See the yellow disk spinning at that energy center. Breathe in and out of the yellow disk.

Slowly focus your attention on the middle of your chest, at your heart. This is the energy center of love. It is green. Spin the green disk with your breath. As your breath expands your lungs and you begin to exhale, feel the greenness of love permeating your body. Return your attention to the disk. Picture the disk opening, like a fan opens, into the shape of a megaphone. The narrow end of the megaphone is attached to your heart. The wide end of the megaphone reaches into the world, beyond the world, to the cosmos. Breathe love into the megaphone. Breathe your love into the world. Use the megaphone to breathe your love into the cosmos.

Now as you inhale, feel love coming back to you. The wide end of the megaphone is catching all the love that is out there and returning it to you. The megaphone works like a funnel. As you breathe in, it pours love into you. With each breath, feel the love travel throughout your body. Let the love of the universe move into your head. Let the love travel down your neck along your spine. Feel the love move from your spine into your arms, into your hands. Feel the love move down your legs, into your feet. Keep breathing. Feel all the love gather in a pool at your feet. With the next breath, draw the love up inside your body, and as you exhale, shower yourself with love. Breathe in and out in the shower of love a few times. Allow your breath to become normal.

Keep your eyes closed and repeat the following affirmations four times:

> *I seek first to understand, then to be understood.*
> *I feel good when I have done something for others.*
> *I am a participant in co-creation through community.*

When you are ready, slowly open your eyes.

Application 4: In Your Own Voice— Continuing Your Journal

Continue your journal by entering any thoughts that come to you as a result of the story, reflections, or applications in this chapter. You might want to think and write about your own connections to community. You may consider how you have put group interests above self interests at work, and what happened at work and to you as a result. Last, try to describe a time when you felt joy in being a part of a group.

Calling

Manny the Millionaire

The Story

Manny was almost dozing off in front of the TV news when they began to read the lottery numbers for that day's pick. The announcer's voice grabbed his attention—22, 3, 14, 11, . . . Were they his numbers? He had come close so often. Even won a couple of the smaller prizes. Barely enough, if that, to cover the fifty dollars' worth of tickets he bought each week. Manny looked over at Rosa. Of course, she wasn't paying any attention to him or the television. She had her nose in a magazine as usual. Very casually, he thought, he got up from his brown leather lounger. He strolled down the hall into the bedroom. Then, his heart pounding, he opened his top bureau drawer and took out the El Producto cigar box he had had since he was a kid. He always used it to hide his treasures. When he was six he hid his marbles, and when he was sixteen the condoms he only hoped he would get the chance to use some day. Now he used it for his lottery tickets. Rosa thought he spent too much on the tickets. She thought he spent too much on everything that was any fun. As he

111

took out the ticket and looked at the numbers—22, 3, 14, 11, . . . he became almost nauseated. They were his numbers, all seven of them. This was it. He had won the big one. Twelve million dollars if there were no other winners.

He could not contain his excitement another minute. He strode into the living room, scooped up his little Rosa in his arms and began a crazy waltz around the room, singing "We're in the Money."

"Put me down this minute, Manny. Are you nuts? What are you singing? 'We're in the Money.' It's more like 'I've Got Plenty of Nothin.'" He kept dancing faster and wilder. "Put me down, you jerk. We're too old for this kind of nonsense." He slowed down but then, unable to restrain his joy, picked up the pace and turned the waltz into his own version of the cha cha twist.

She squirmed away from him and plunked herself back down on the couch. "Okay, what's going on?" Some new hare-brained scheme to own the racetrack? Or have you taken a permanent home on the 18th hole at Pine Ridge?"

"Rosa," Manny sat down next to her, leaning forward to look into her face. "For once, just listen and don't say anything. We have just won the lottery."

"So, the lottery," she sneered. "How much this time, fifty?—a big one, five hundred? Look what you spend every week on your lottery, your track, your golf, your dinners where we pay for all your freeloader friends."

He took her hands. "Just listen. We won the big one. It's twelve million if we are the only winners. We can do everything. We can have everything both of us, either of us, have ever wanted. I know sometimes when I'm spending money having a good time, you worry about the bills. It may have been close, but we've always managed to pay them. I have had a decent-paying job at SeeBrighter Electronics and . . ."

Okay, so you've been director of personnel, but it seems to me, you've really been the director of parties. You know, sometimes I just wish you would have given me the money for the month's bills instead of one more surprise at a fancy restaurant with a gift I really didn't want."

"But Rosa, why are you bringing up all this old stuff? Listen to me. Whatever happens next, we are rich, or, as the rich would say, we are now comfortable—for life."

"If this is really true, tell me the story when you show me the bank book."

Manny was indeed the only lottery winner for that night. He turned in his ticket and set up a bank account for himself and Rosa. Manny did like to play. He often said to his friends, "Work is interfering with my life." Now, he thought, he would just quit his job. Golf, the horses, and good times were all his. But he had not been in personnel for nothing. He would not be a fool in his last weeks there. The company owed him twelve weeks vacation, which he planned to use up before submitting his resignation.

On the last day before his vacation, Manny decided to play it straight at work. He had always enjoyed his job and he was going to give them a day's work for a day's pay. He went into the office hugging his secret wealth to himself. He helped his clients, a bunch of young guys and gals who were applying for slots in the company's internal management development program. He really liked to see the good ones make progress and worked hard with them on their résumés, applications, and interview skills. One of his favorites, Garcia, a good-looking kid who reminded him of himself when he was thirty, came in. Garcia had all the technical skills and the right look, but he still needed help answering the kind of questions he would face in an interview. Manny got so wrapped up in helping Garcia that he forgot he was leaving and made an appointment for the following week.

In the weeks that followed, Manny was a free man. He slept late. He read the paper slowly. He bought the sporty new car he'd been longing for. But he didn't get in as much golf as he thought he would. Most of his friends were at work during the new playtimes that he had. Going to the track was okay, but less fun by himself, and winning wasn't as much fun when there was no danger in losing. He even missed Rosa's nagging. She seemed not to care when he bought lottery tickets or spent money in ways that she used to resent.

He tried to spend more time with Rosa. He took her out to lunch, to dinner, to breakfast. Rosa said she was getting too fat. They flew to Spain for a week. Rosa said it was too hot there. And from her point of view, she stressed, bullfights were worse than horse races.

One day, just after lunch, Manny roamed aimlessly around the house and yard. Coming into the living room, he sighed and plopped down in his lounger, across from Rosa on the couch. To Rosa he seemed so much sadder than he had before he'd won the lottery.

"Manny," she said, looking over her magazine, "I know you're a millionaire, but I think you need a job."

"What do you mean, 'a job'? What would I need a job for? We have all the money we need."

"Yes, but every time you came home from the office, you always seemed so bouncy, so happy. Sometimes you were so happy, it really bugged me."

"Well, I was happy at the office. I had my friends. And you know, I really liked figuring out how to help some of the people I worked with. You know the last day I was there, I was so crazy, that I forgot I was leaving and made an appointment for the next week?"

"Maybe that's it. You didn't tell anyone you were quitting. Why not just forget that you were leaving?"

"Rosa, tell me the truth. Is it really that you don't like me anymore, that you don't want me around so much? Please, tell me."

"Manny, I know sometimes I sound angry. And sometimes I am angry. But you know, we have been together for more than thirty years. I'm not going anywhere. My life is with you. But your life is not only with me. It's with your work as well, with the people there and what you do for them."

Career Issues

In the story, Manny faced three questions:

▮ How did his desire for fun and his desire for work come together?

▮ What did he really want to get out of life?

▮ What experiences that made him happy was he missing when he no longer went to work?

Here are some related career issues that many people face:

▮ Identifying the skills and knowledge we possess and enjoy using at work

▮ Identifying interests in work and in life

▮ Understanding how our personality characteristics affect our behavior at work

▮ Understanding how values affect choice of work

▮ Knowing what we are called to do in life

Reflections

In this story, Manny was a person who liked to have fun. He was a good-time kind of guy. A lot of his fun seemed related to taking chances—betting on the races, buying lottery tickets. However, the enjoyment really came from his companionship with the

Finding your calling is about finding your ideal work.

other people involved in the activities, from being with his buddies at the race track, from walking the links with his golfing companions, and even from listening to Rosa's carping. Manny was a true extrovert, a person who got his energy from being with others. What he did not recognize, until Rosa brought him the message, was that he was equally energized by these interpersonal relationships at work. In personnel work, Manny had found his ideal job.

Finding your calling is about finding your ideal work. Sometimes we think of a calling or a vocation as being limited to religious occupations. But *calling* really means recognizing the gifts you have and using them in any productive work. *Gifts* is another word for interests, skills, and abilities. When you recognize your gifts and use them, you are answering your call. And when you answer your call, you sense the strong connection between yourself and your work. Often this sense of connection between yourself and your work leads to a generalized sense of well-being in all aspects of life.

Sometimes we don't recognize the setting in which we are answering our calling. This is what happened to Manny when he tried to leave his job. He did not realize how much joy he derived from his work and how central it was to his happiness. He thought his happiness came from his leisure activities, his playtime. But when he had only playtime and all the money he would ever need to play, he had a sense of emptiness. The sense of emptiness did not come from the loss of a paying job. It came from the loss of carrying out the functions of the job. Those functions were Manny's answer to his calling. We are not saying that the only route to happiness is a paying job, but that the way to happiness is finding meaningful work in the world consistent with your gifts, whether or not that work is for pay.

The energy center for this chapter is the one located at the throat. It is associated with speech, communication, and all expression. Calling is not just about identifying what is within us. It is about expressing what we hear through every means of communication—verbal and nonverbal—that we have. It is about listening and doing. In the Bible, God commands: "You shall hear and you shall do."

People who answer their calling feel what some have identified as "bliss" and others as "flow." We will begin by examining what is meant by bliss and flow. We will then discuss how gifts—interests, knowledge, skills, personality characteristics, and val-

The way to happiness is finding meaningful work in the world consistent with your gifts, whether or not that work is for pay.

ues—connect to answering the calling that leads to bliss and flow. Throughout the reflections you will find ways to identify your own calling and how to answer it. The sections of these reflections include:

- How It Feels to Answer Your Calling

- Knowing Your Life Calling: Interests, Knowledge, and Skills

- Knowing Your Life Calling: Personality, Characteristics, and Values

How It Feels to Answer Your Calling

The general feeling that one has when doing work that answers a calling is a sense of oneness with the work itself and with everything associated with it. Poet Donald Hall has called this "absorbedness." In his book *Life Work* (1993), he described his "best day." "The best day begins with waking early—I check the clock: damn! it's only 3:00 A.M.—because I want so much to get out of bed and start working. Usually something particular beckons so joyously—like a poem that I have good hope for, that seems to go well. Will it look as happy today as it looked yesterday?" Almost agonizing over the delay, he exquisitely painted his impatience to get out of bed, the coffee making, the details of the morning until he finished breakfast reading the paper. And then, he wrote, "As I approach the end of the *Globe*, saving the sports section until last, I feel work-excitement building, job-pressure mounting—until I need resist it no more but sit at the desk and open the folder that holds the day's beginning, its desire and its

The general feeling that one has when doing work that answers a calling is a sense of oneness with the work itself and with everything associated with it.

hope. Then I lose myself. In the best part of the best day, *absorbedness* occupies me from footsole to skulltop."

What Donald Hall calls "absorbedness" has been called "flow" by psychologist Mihaly Csikszentmihalyi (1990). "'Flow' is the way people describe their state of mind when consciousness is harmoniously ordered and they want to pursue whatever they are doing for its own sake." The word *flow* in its ordinary usage suggests continuous or unbroken movement, the flowing of a river or stream. It suggests an outpouring of water or energy. That continuous outpouring of work with no sense of beginning or ending or separation of worker and work is what is meant by Csikszentmihalyi. Furthermore, Csikszentmihalyi found that flow is not limited to some higher order of jobs or to Western experience. He wrote, "One can find flow in the most unlikely places, in the most humble jobs of daily life."

Absorbedness—the sense people have when they are seamlessly connected to their work—is the same as flow. And it is the same as what Joseph Campbell (Campbell & Moyers, 1988) has called "bliss." He urges people to follow their bliss. "If you follow your bliss, you put yourself on a kind of track that has been there all the while, waiting for you, and the life that you ought to be living is the one that you are living. Wherever you are—if you are following your bliss, you are enjoying refreshment, that life within you, all the time."

One common definition of *bliss* is "spiritual joy." So when you hear your calling and respond by doing the work to which you are called, you experience flow, absorbedness, and bliss—or spiritual joy. The longing for this joy has been expressed by another poet, Robert Frost (1949b). In the poem "Two Tramps in Mud-Time," Frost described the arrival of two strangers who come to his farm and offer to split wood. Although the narrator of the poem loves the task himself, particularly on the day in early spring when the tramps appear, he recognizes that he is playing at something that is the work of others for pay. He hires the strangers because of their need, but not without some reluctance, and it is in that reluctance that he recognizes his calling. "My object in life is to unite / My avocation and my vocation / As my two eyes make one in sight." Frost uses the word *avocation* to mean calling and he uses the word *vocation* to mean his job. If he can follow his calling in his job, his spiritual joy will be complete.

Finally, in *Zen and the Art of Motorcycle Maintenance*, Robert Pirsig (1974) describes the mechanic absorbed in his work and gives us the ordinary words we use for the sense of oneness with our work. He describes it as "'Being with it,' 'being a natural,' 'taking hold.'"

Calling is feeling the harmonious connection to whatever you are doing, to the tools of the work, and to the people with whom you work. There may well be a sense that if you have been called to the work you are doing, then you are helping to create the universe itself. And through all of this may be the pervasive feeling that what you are doing is good in a general sense, of a high quality, and ethically right.

Knowing Your Life Calling:
Interests, Knowledge, and Skills

In days of yore, according to legend (see Barber, 1961), after King Uther Pendragon died there was evil and intrigue afoot in the land. People were vying for power; many claimed to be king. But the power to be king rested in a sword that was embedded in a stone. Only the rightful king could remove the sword. To everyone's amazement, a young man, Arthur, removed the sword and became the noble king who ruled over the land of Camelot and the knights of the Round Table. Merlin, the magician, revealed the source of Arthur's strength. He was a true, if illegitimate, son of King Pendragon. He was called to remove the sword and he had been given the unique ability, or gift, to be able to do so.

How can you recognize your unique abilities? Certainly there is no Merlin waiting in the wings to identify your birthright. But you are carrying that birthright within you, cast—in modern terms—as interests, knowledge, and skills. An *interest* is an internal state that gives you joy or satisfaction in an activity. *Skills* are those things a person is capable of doing as a result of talent, training, or a combination of both. *Knowledge* is different from skill. First, it is not innate; it is learned. Second, it generally requires the acquistion and personal reframing of information. While there are a number of instruments that attempt to measure interests, skills, and knowledge separately, for the adult seeking self-knowledge about calling, the important point is the junction where all three come together. That is, calling includes the utilization of skills and knowledge where they are also motivated by interest.

One way of looking at your interests, skills, and knowledge is to examine them as relative preferences for working with people, data, or things. Another way of examining your preferences is to consider them in terms of six categories of activity: realistic, investigative, artistic, social, enterprising, and conventional. We will look at how you can use each of these classification schemes to identify your own abilities.

For many years, the United States Department of Labor classified the activities of all occupations into three categories: data, people, and things.

■ The occupational activities related to *data* involve the ability to compare, copy, compute, compile, analyze, coordinate, and synthesize. Working with data includes any tasks related to numbers, symbols, or detailed facts.

■ The occupational activities related to *people* involve the ability to take instructions, serve, speak, signal, divert, supervise, instruct, and mentor. Working with people includes direct service to others in fields as varied as education, health, sales, and hospitality.

■ The occupational activities related to *things* include the ability to handle, feed into machinery, tend, manipulate, operate or control, do precision work, and set up. Working with things includes any tasks that require the manipulation of objects or tools, whether the tools are the delicate instruments of surgery or massive hydraulic lifts.

Twenty thousand occupations in the United States were analyzed. For each occupation, the relative amount of skill, from lowest to highest, in each of the three categories—data, people, things—was assessed. For example, the occupation of physician requires the highest skills in all three areas. However, a pathologist—a physician who works only in the laboratory—requires the highest skills only in data and things.

One way you can assess your interests, knowledge, and skills is to consider how much you like working with data, how much with people, and how much with things. Then, you can also consider how much you know and how skilled you are in each of those aspects of work. Your calling will come from occupations whose requirements correspond to the level of knowledge, skill, and interest that you possess. Of course, if you have the interest, you may also decide to acquire the knowledge and skills needed. In our story, Manny was definitely a "people" person. He particularly liked helping, or mentoring, the younger workers. He gained his bliss from using the skills and knowledge he had developed.

The second way to examine your interests, skills, and knowledge is to use the six categories of interest and six matching categories of occupational environment. This categorization scheme was developed by John Holland (1985), who wrote, "People search for environments that will let them exercise their skills and abilities, express their attitudes and values, and take on agreeable problems and roles." Here is how each of the six categories of people and their related occupations are described.

- Realistic people, who are generally frank, practical, and persistent, often like jobs such as automobile mechanic, electrician, or aircraft controller. Such people generally have mechanical ability but may lack social skills.

- Investigative people, who are generally analytical, cautious, curious, and rational, often like jobs such as biologist, chemist, or medical technologist. Such people often have mathematical and scientific ability but may lack leadership ability.

- Artistic people, who are generally complicated, emotional, expressive, and imaginative, often like jobs such as musician, stage director, actor, or writer. Such people often have artistic ability but lack clerical skills.

- Social people, who are generally empathic, friendly, helpful, and idealistic, often like jobs such as teacher, counselor, or social worker. Such people often have social skills but lack mathematical ability.

- Enterprising people, who are generally adventurous, excitement-seeking, extroverted, and talkative, often like jobs such as salesperson, manager, and business executive. Such people often have leadership skills but lack scientific ability.

- Conventional people, who are generally conforming, conscientious, methodical, and obedient, often like jobs such as bookkeeper, financial analyst, and word processor. Such people often have arithmetic skills but lack artistic ability.

John Holland has developed a widely used instrument, the *Self-Directed Search,* to help people find the occupations that most closely fit their personalities as described above. As part of the instrument, Holland (1994) suggests a method for identifying interests, a method that you can use. Make a list of the occupations you most frequently daydream about. Don't edit the list according to skills you believe you presently have or don't have. Don't edit out occupations that you feel are too farfetched for you to reach. When you have the inclusive list, see which categories you most frequently identify with in your daydreams. Most people find that some combination of categories comes closest to describing their career interests. In our story, Manny was a combination of social and enterprising. He was friendly, helpful, and empathic. That is, he liked working and playing with people. That was his social side. His enterprising side came out in his excitement-seeking in leisure activities, but it also came out in his leadership at work. He had risen to the position of director of personnel. Once you have identified your category or combination of categories, you have a key to your gifts and you are closer to identifying your calling.

While we have provided some brief instructions on how to identify your abilities, we recognize that it is not an easy task. Robert Frost (1949a) described a young man who leans into a well and always sees himself unclearly in the water. Then one day a pebble falls in the water and the water clears for an instant, and in that instant he sees himself clearly, "For once, then, something." Of course, once the ripples caused by the pebble are gone, the water is murky once more. Like Frost's young man, we must keep looking into our personal wells, examining our depths, and searching for the moments of enlightenment that show us our calling. Once we have found the calling, it is important that we not hide our talents from ourselves or others.

One young woman we know was a reading specialist in the public school system. While she was able to work effectively with individual students, she found herself unable to speak up clearly at team meetings. She knew she had valuable information about students, but she was so anxious about how she would appear to other members of the team that she would actually stammer when she tried to express her ideas. This made her even more anxious. She realized that she was not only hiding her own talents but depriving her students of full service when she could not bring their needs to the meetings. Through introspection and the help of a therapist, she was able to refocus her attention from herself to others. She was able to use her gifts and return the favor of her gifts by being fully invested in her work.

Knowing Your Life Calling: Personality Characteristics and Values

In the last section we looked at gifts as a way of knowing our calling. Another aspect of our calling comes from our personality characteristics. First we will look at how the theory of personality types developed by Carl Jung (1933/1931) is related to calling. Then we will see how values, another aspect of our personalities, are also a part of this picture.

Carl Jung linked personality theory and work. In earlier chapters, we talked about the difference between the extroverted and introverted personalities. We did not use the common definition of *extrovert* as outgoing, the life of the party; or of *introvert* as a stay-at-home wallflower. We used Jung's definitions. The extrovert is the person who gains energy from being with others. The introvert recovers energy by activities carried out alone. Jung called these *attitudes*. He also described four functions of the personality. These are thinking, feeling, sensing, and intuition.

Thinking and feeling are rational functions. They describe the basis upon which people tend to make decisions. People who prefer to exercise the function of thinking tend to make their judgments based on abstract principles. These people tend to use logic, analysis, and principles of policy and justice when making decisions. On the other hand, people who prefer to exercise the function of feeling tend to make their judgments based on personal values. They tend to use impact on people, sympathy, and mercy when making decisions.

For example, suppose a person has to make budget cuts in personnel in a company, or "downsize." The thinking person will probably first analyze the company's needs and policies before making a decision. That person will probably also consider such things as seniority and affirmative action because of a concern for justice. The feeling person will probably first consider the impact on individuals and might look at who can best afford to be laid off, and who is most likely to get a new job. However, mature individuals are aware of both functions, and while they may start their analysis with the preferred function, they will incorporate considerations of both thinking and feeling in a final decision. In our illustration, certainly considerations of policy and justice along with considerations of personal impact are appropriate.

Sensing and intuition are perceptive functions. They describe the basis upon which people tend to receive information. People who are sensing concern themselves with facts, details, and specifics. People who are intuitive concern themselves with meaning, patterns, and possibilities.

When sensing people tackle a new subject, for example, they prefer to read a textbook from beginning to end, pausing as needed to digest the specifics of information. Intuitive people, tackling the same subject and using the same text, tend to skim the table of contents and search for the main ideas. The sensing person may miss the "big picture," and the intuitive person may never absorb the details. However, mature individuals are aware of both functions and, while they may start with the preferred function, they will incorporate both sensing and intuition in a quest for knowledge that is important to them. So the sensing person will make an effort to step back from the details to find the patterns or major themes of a book, and the intuitive person will make an effort to incorporate the details into the patterns.

Where does Manny fit in this scheme? First, he is clearly an extrovert. His attention is focused toward people and actions. He is energized by being with others and has many friends and colleagues. In decision making, Manny is a feeling person. He is so wrapped up in his empathy with the young Garcia that he makes an appointment to see him even after he himself no longer plans to be at work. He responds to winning the lottery with a great deal of emotion. He swings his wife off her feet and they go off on a whirlwind of vacations. However, Manny is not all feeling. He does not quit his job impulsively, but takes the vacation time owed him. This is perfectly appropriate and mature behavior for a person who prefers his feeling function but who has learned to recognize the importance of objective logic when he needs it. When it comes to sensing versus intuition, he is highly intuitive. He relies on his hunches, on luck, and possibilities. In his personal life he seems to have little use for facts or details. But at work he again shows both sides. He could not have risen to the position of director of personnel without some attention to detail.

When you look at the functions, you may be tempted to place values on them, to rate one as "better" than the other. Jung made it perfectly clear that these functions are equally valuable and equally natural. As the old folk song goes, "All God's children's got a place in the choir, some sing low, some sing higher, some sing loud on the telephone wire." The purpose in identifying your functions is so you can know yourself better and understand how your personality is related to your calling.

One way you can identify your preferred functions is to reflect on the definitions of the functions and your behavior in recent situations at work or elsewhere. Jung believed that we are born with our preferred functions and that we can identify them through our behavior. You can also ask other people you trust about how they see your behavior in terms of type. If you want to get more specific information, you can take the *Myers-Briggs Type Indicator*® (1998) or read the book *Gifts Differing* (Myers with Myers, 1995/ 1980). Both the instrument and the book are based on Jung's theory of personality types.

Values are a function of personality. Mark Savickas (1997) defined values as "general goals that confirm who we are and what we wish to become. They signal a commitment to a way of life." There are many values related to career issues, and those values concern such major questions as the rewards we wish to receive from work, the settings in which we prefer to work, and the kinds of people we most like to work with.

All of the previous information you developed about your calling must now be looked at in the light of values. It stands to reason that you will gain greater satisfaction from a position compatible with your interests and abilities than from an incompati-

Values are the prisms through which all self-information passes, and they are the filter through which all decisions are crystallized. They can anchor you in place or move you to the ends of the earth.

ble one. For example, if you decided that your interests, skills, and knowledge best suited you for a career in teaching, you would not necessarily be happy teaching in any school or organization. You would be happiest teaching in that organization whose values are closest to your own. As another example, you might not accept a promotion or pay raise if it meant you had to leave the area in which your children were happily engaged in school and neighborhood activities.

Values are the prisms through which all self-information passes, and they are the filter through which all decisions are crystallized. They can anchor you in place or move you to the ends of the earth. How can you identify your own core values? First, you can make a list of those things you would not sacrifice for any career move. They might include health, love, friendship, learning, faith, or relationships with particular people or places. Second, you might ask yourself what circumstances at work would cause you to put your job on the line. These might include moral values, working conditions, or social relations.

Each value does not exist by itself. Values only exist in relation to each other. If we were to give you a list of the core values identified by most people, you would probably say, "Yes, those are my values too." However, the true worth of a value comes into play when we must choose between one good and another. For example, try prioritizing the following six values to see which is of greatest importance to you, remembering that all of them are probably important: beauty, family, high income, independence, love, security. Now imagine that the order you choose means that you will have in your life more of the value you put first and none of the value you put last. Can you make your list easily?

Viktor Frankl (1967, 1972, 1992/1963), a psychiatrist whose writing was influenced by his experiences in the concentration camps of Nazi Germany, concluded that there are three broad categories of value. The first category is "creative values." These are found in productive work. The second category is "experiential values." These are known through the enjoyment of the good and beautiful in life. The final category is "attitudinal values." These are values that go beyond or are outside of all experience. Attitudinal values give unique meaning to life even in the face of suffering. Frankl believed that the loss of all values equals the loss of meaning in life.

In the story, Manny lost sight of his values when he planned to quit his job. He strongly valued helping others, but when he won the lottery, he thought that a life of play would more than make up for the expression of that value. It did not take long for him to recognize how important this was to him. The wise person in his life, his wife, Rosa, recognized how important using his gifts was to Manny. When she said, "Your life is with work, with the people there, and what you do for them," Rosa identified Manny's calling for him. She knew that Manny had the gifts to help others, and more than merely having the gifts, he valued how he used them in the help he gave.

In his work, Manny embodied the self he hoped to be. Ask yourself: "Who is the self I hope to be?"

Calling and Spirituality—
Some Concluding Thoughts

Calling is about hearing your own song and singing it out loud and clear. We hear our calling by exploring our interests, skills, knowledge, personalities, and values. We sing our song by expressing ourselves in the productive work that reflects our calling.

Calling begins with listening and ends with singing. Many spiritual traditions embrace practices that foster inner stillness so that we may hear. We hear in order to do. We do in order to sing. Bruce Chatwin (1987) followed aboriginal holy people in their "walkabouts" in Australia. He concluded that the paths they were walking were their songlines, and that songs are the first expression of spirituality. You cannot sing for others until you find your voice. That is your first calling.

Calling is about hearing your own song and singing it out loud and clear. We hear our calling by exploring our interests, skills, knowledge, personalities, and values.

Applications

In this chapter we looked at the relationships among calling, spirituality, and work. We also looked at how we can find our calling by exploring aspects of ourselves that include our gifts, our personality, and our values. The applications that follow are designed to help you in four ways:

▪ To discover some of your long-term interests and related skills

▪ To clarify your values

▪ To strengthen your appreciation of yourself

▪ To increase your feeling of bliss, flow, or absorbedness

Application 1: My Favorite Toy

In this exercise you will look back on your earliest memories of a favorite toy, game, or activity. By examining these memories, you will be able to see how your earliest interests are still active in your life today. You may also see that skills you played at having are now skills you really have developed or would like to develop.

One person we know, for example, remembered playing detective. She would don an outfit she thought of as her detective clothes—boots and a cape. She had, she reported, "a big magnifying glass like Sherlock Holmes." Armed with these, she went into the alley behind her house and down the block on which she lived. She peered through her magnifying glass and gathered letters. Since she was too young to read, she decided that the letters were in code and she took them home to decode them. Today, she earns her living as a forensic psychiatrist. She uncovers the psychological clues in people's lives for complicated court cases and "decodes" responses to various tests.

Directions: On a piece of paper, draw the earliest toys you remember playing with. These toys do not have to be purchased items. They can be buttons, string, empty cans. They can be any objects that were your objects of play. In our example, the toys would be the cape, the boots, the glass, and the "coded" notes.

On the reverse side of your paper, describe how you enjoyed playing with your toy. You may write about others if they were involved in your play, but you don't have to include others. Just try to be as true to your memories as you can.

When you have finished drawing the toys and describing how you played with them, complete the four worksheets of "My Favorite Toy."

My Favorite Toy

---

1. Consider the activities you carried out in playing with your favorite toy, and list them in the appropriate categories that follow.

Data

People

Things

Realistic

Investigative

Artistic

Social

Enterprising

Conventional

2. Now look at the same categories and consider your work and other activities today. List the activities that show continuing interests or skills in their appropriate categories.

Data

People

Things

Realistic

Investigative

Artistic

Social

Enterprising

Conventional

3. Compare your lists. Are there any categories of interests, skills, and knowledge that you enjoyed as a child and that you have let slip away? How might you resume your interest or skills in this area if you want to do so?

4. Using the information developed in response to items 1–3, complete the following matrix. In the first column, place a check mark next to each category in which you had interests, skills, or knowledge as a child. (Remember to think as a child thinks: If you believed you knew something, you knew it, even if the knowledge was incorrect or the skill was "just pretend.") In the second column, place a check mark next to each category in which you have interests, skills, and knowledge today. In the third column, place a check mark in the categories in which you no longer display your early gifts but would like to resume doing so. And in the last column, check those categories that may have interested you as a child, but which

Category	Childhood Gifts	Adult Gifts	Gifts to Be Redeveloped	Gifts to Be Returned
Data				
People				
Things				
Realistic				
Investigative				
Artistic				
Social				
Enterprising				
Conventional				

Application 2: The Values Store

In this exercise, you will clarify your values by making choices that force you to select some values and leave others behind.

Directions: *In doing this exercise it is important that you do not read ahead but carry out each step one by one. We know this only tempts you to read ahead, but try not to.*

The Values Store

---

1. You have entered the Values Store. The merchandise is made up of eighteen values. You have a $500 budget and want every item in the store. But the manager says each value costs $100, and you may select any five you want. In Column 1 of the chart on page 132, place a dollar sign next to each value you decide to purchase. Remember, you are only allowed five items.

   Do not read Direction 2 until you have completed Direction 1.

2. Just as you are leaving the store, the owner comes running after you. You have purchased the exact set of values the owner promised earlier to another customer. The owner knows you want the values but as a compromise offers you $1,000 each for any of your values. If you sell one value, you can buy two from the remaining list. And if you sell two of your original values, you can buy four new ones. And so on. You will never be able to get the values you sold back again. If you agree to sell any of the values, draw a line through the dollar sign you placed in Column 1 of the chart, and choose the correct number of additional values by placing dollar signs in Column 2.

3. Look over the list of values you returned. Do you have any regrets? If you do, place a sad face or a tear in Column 3.

Values	Column 1	Column 2	Column 3
Adventure			
Culture			
Family			
Freedom			
Health			
Helping others			
High income			
Independence			
Leadership			
Leisure			
Love			
Nature			
Prestige			
Productivity			
Religion			
Security			
Success			
Variety			

Application 3: A Love Song

People tend to give themselves negative messages. Research shows that 95 percent of the messages we give ourselves are negative. We call ourselves stupid, clumsy, lazy, and slow. We are far harder on ourselves than we would dare to be on others. How often do we look in the mirror and admire the bright, shiny face we see? This exercise is about singing and about sending yourself a positive message.

Directions: Select a love song—popular, folk, classical, hymn—and sing or hum it to yourself every night before you go to sleep and in the morning for one week. Each morning record how you feel in your journal.

If you don't know any love song that you would like to sing, then make one up to any familiar tune. For example, take the childhood song that goes, "The farmer in the dell, the farmer in the dell. Heigh ho the derry-o, the farmer in the dell." Instead of the original words, sing, "I know I look so well, I know I feel so swell. Heigh ho the merry-o, my work will really jell."

The words to the song I will sing to myself this week:

Application 4: A Meditation on Calling

Directions: You may want to ask someone else to read this slowly to you or you may want to read the meditation into a tape recorder for yourself before you begin. This meditation begins like all the others with directions that will put you in a receptive frame of mind and spirit.

Sit in a comfortable chair with a firm back, or on the floor with your back straight and your legs crossed comfortably. Place your hands on your thighs, palms up and slightly open.

Straighten yourself as if you were about to pay attention. Now let your shoulders drop naturally. Breathe slowly in through your nose and out through your mouth. You may make a sound with your breath as you exhale. That's fine. Just breathe in and out deeply and evenly for a few moments. Let your breath return to normal.

Begin to feel the power of the earth wherever your body is in contact with the floor or chair. Maintain your contact with the abundant power of the physical, material world. Let the energy of the brown and red earth, its dryness, its moist fertility enter your body. Keep the earth's energy within you. At the same time, become aware of the top of your head. Imagine you can feel the electricity of all the spirit in the cosmos. As you draw in one breath, draw in the abundance of the earth. Exhale. As you draw in the next breath, draw in the light of the cosmos. Picture this as you breathe in and out. Any time you lose your concentration in the exercise, just return to your breathing.

Move your attention to the first energy center, the one at the base of your spine. See the red disk spinning at that energy center. Breathe in and out of the red disk several times.

Now move your attention to your pelvis. Picture an orange disk spinning around your pelvis. This is the energy of your second energy center. Breathe into the orange disk.

Move your attention to the third energy center at your midsection. See the yellow disk spinning at that energy center. Breathe in and out of the yellow disk.

Now focus your attention on the middle of your chest, at your heart. See the green disk of this energy center. Spin the green disk with your breath.

Slowly move your attention to your throat. Picture a blue disk spinning at your throat. This is the energy center of communication. Breathe in and out of the blue disk. Keep the blue disk spinning. As you breathe in, feel blueness permeate your body. Feel the blue energy enter you from your toes to your head. Keep the blue disk spinning as you breath in and out. Picture notes of music emanating from your throat. Your whole throat is surrounded by music. Let the music expand and surround your chest. Let the music grow bigger so that it covers your whole body. Let the music grow even bigger so that both your body and your head are surrounded by notes of the most beautiful music. This is the music of your calling. You can hear the music. You know your calling. You are not only hearing the music, you are the maker of the music. As you hear the music, and play the music, and sing the music, you experience the bliss of your wonderful song. Keep playing the music of your song. Breathe in and out of the blue disk for a few more moments.

Keep your eyes closed and repeat the following affirmation four times.

I can hear the work I am called to do.

When you are ready, slowly open your eyes.

Application 5: In Your Own Voice— Continuing Your Journal

In addition to the activities that you did in the Applications section, there were many opportunities for reflection in this chapter. You may want to continue your journal by noting your observations on your interests, skills, knowledge, personality type, and values. You may also want to reflect on how these are expressed in the work you do and in other areas of your life. Look for evidence of your gifts. Write down every compliment you are given, no matter how perfunctory you believe the comment is. Look for moments of absorbedness, bliss, or flow. Can you identify your calling? Remember to keep writing and rereading your journal.

Harmony

David in the Dollhouse

The Story

"Can I help you?" David called to the woman who was next in line at reception.

"Yes, I checked in late last night and I want to make sure you have my room reservations for the next two nights. The name is Garson, Shirley Garson." She smiled, almost apologetically. "There have just been too many times lately that things have gotten fouled up. I'm not blaming computers. Even though I am a member of the 'older generation,' I work with them myself. But there seems to be more error now than there used to be. Maybe I've grown less tolerant. When you get to be my age, you have the right to be concerned with your own comfort, to be a bit of a grouch."

Shirley said all this with such a pleasant smile, that David could not help but respond. "You're right about foul-ups. I'm only twenty-five and I find myself getting annoyed at them—you know the whole world out there seems to go wrong some days. Let me check," and he bent to the computer keyboard and screen that held the information for La Poupée, the San Francisco flagship hotel for the deluxe Rainbow Hotel chain. "You have a double room for the next two nights. Non-smoking. And by the way, you're not a grouch. You should hear—or maybe you shouldn't hear—some of the things people say at this desk. And this is a well-run hotel. So, comparatively speaking, you're no grouch. But, is there anything else I can do for you?

"Thanks," Shirley said, "nothing right now." She smiled once more. He seemed a really pleasant young man. And she walked away from the desk toward the elevators.

"Can I help you?" David called to the next person in line. He again donned his pleasant, hotel-trained smile.

"The name is Evans. Reservation for two. Two queen beds."

Once again David bent to the computer. The reservation was in order. He offered the check-in form to Mr. Evans. Mr. Evans wordlessly signed and returned it. David thanked him and asked the routine question, "Is there anything else I can do for you?"

David looked toward the check-in line. It was going to be a quiet day. There was no one waiting for him or for Judy, the other front desk clerk.

"How're you doing, Judy?" he asked as he walked toward her station behind the high marble counter. This was a regular part of their morning routine whenever the flow of customer traffic allowed.

She sighed, "I never know whether I prefer these quiet days or the busy ones. What do you like better? Bored or frantic?"

He was about to give her one of his flip answers, the kind of light banter they usually had, when he realized he really didn't like either kind of day any longer. Both bored him. Being busy left him no time to think and being quiet left him with time for too many thoughts.

"Judy, how did you get into this racket?"

"David, you already know. We talked about this last week. I needed a job for a few weeks when I first got to San Francisco, and here I've been for one year, four months, and three weeks."

David barely heard her answer. He counted back and realized that the temporary job he had taken had now lasted five years. He had come to the Rainbow Corporation straight out of San Francisco City College.

He looked up to check the line. The reflexes of the job were always in place. Check the line. Smile. Greet the customer. Find out their request. Smile. Fulfill their request. Smile. Hope it wasn't one of the real grouches who insisted on seeing a manager. Smile again. And send them on their way—with a smile, of course. Check the line. Smile. With the thought of the word *smile*, David found himself smiling at his own thoughts. He had taken the job because he thought it would satisfy two desires that were otherwise incompatible. He really wanted to be an actor, and he really wanted security. He had seen the front desk job as an acting job. He saw the routine of greeting people as a script. He saw the need to smile and be pleasant regardless of his own inner feelings on a particular day as acting, and he saw his response to the variety in customers as improvisation. In fact, he had heard that at the Disney hotels they even called all the workers "members of the cast."

David looked at his watch. Eleven, time for his morning break. David had a secret addiction—not coffee, cigarettes, or anything ingestible or inhalable. His addiction was the hotel store. The store carried out the theme of the hotel. It was stocked with dolls. And here was David's secret: dollhouses complete with miniature furniture and tiny figures. Every break, David went to the collection of dollhouses. He saw each of them as a stage set on which he performed the leading role. There was the Victorian dollhouse decorated for Christmas. He was, of course, Tiny Tim. There was the sumptuous palace. He could never decide whether he was King Lear (maybe too young for that role), Hamlet, or the prince in any one of several fairy tales he remembered as he drifted off in front of the dollhouses. He seemed to like playing kings. Another favorite was the pagoda dollhouse in which he was definitely the King of Siam waiting for one of his wives or Anna.

"Hi, David, isn't it?" He was wakened from his reverie by the voice of Mrs. Garson.

"Hi, Mrs. Garson. How's your day going?"

"It's fine. But please call me Shirley. I love these dollhouses. I guess you like them too. It's probably stereotyping, but I wouldn't expect a young guy like you to find them as fascinating as I do. However, you really seemed wrapped up in looking at that one," pointing to the pagoda.

"Yes, they are special to me. How about you? Did you just wander in or do you particularly like dollhouses?"

"I love dollhouses, have since I was a kid. But they also represent a kind of unfinished part of my life. When I was very little, five or six, my grandparents had a dollhouse for me. And my grandmother, who was very talented in sewing, crocheting— all kinds of needlework—had custom-decorated the house. Not only was all the furniture upholstered, but, believe it or not, my dollhouse had a crocheted, brown toilet-seat cover and matching bathroom rug with my initials worked in yellow. For so long, I wanted a granddaughter so that I could do the same thing for her that my grandmother did for me. However, I have two sons and two grandsons, whom I adore, but it has never seemed the right time. I didn't feel I had the right audience for a doll- house."

"It's funny that you should use the word 'audience.' I really want to be an actor and I picture myself as an actor playing a role as I look at each dollhouse. In fact, when I took the job here at Rainbow Hotels, I really wanted an acting job. I studied acting in community college. I got rave reviews in student productions. My profs encouraged me and got me a summer theater job. It was just a small role, but everyone said I did very well. But, what kept haunting me even then was the struggle. I knew that other actors, except for those who make it really big, don't really have a secure livelihood. But it's secure here. That's why I stay. Some- times I think of it as the velvet claws of the Rainbow chain."

"Velvet claws, what a wonderful metaphor and horrible image. Isn't there anything in between? A job where you could be acting or using some of those abilities but also get some secu- rity in the long run?"

"Well, I don't think you can have both at the same time. I have taken all the interest tests. They all point to acting.

"But what about you? Why don't you furnish a dollhouse? You really seem to want to do it."

"I don't know. Sometimes you want to do something and the right time to do it just seems to come—and then to go—before you even knew it was there."

David suddenly realized the time. He thanked Shirley for the conversation and went back to finish his workday. That night, images of the dollhouses and Shirley drifted across his mind as he fell asleep. He dreamed he was in a dollhouse that looked like the hotel lobby, and Shirley was there with him as his costar in a great drama. Looking down on the dollhouse were his parents, frowning as they often did in real life. In the drama of the dream, he said, "I am an actor and I act." Shirley said, "Sometimes you want to do something and the right time to do it just seems to come—and then to go—before you even knew it was there. I'm glad you know this is the time for you." And in the dream, he saw his parents drift off, losing shape, like clouds on a sunny day.

In the morning, David awoke far happier than he had been for a long while. He went to his desk and took out the application for the actors' studio that his drama teacher had recommended five years earlier. He knew he had a lot to learn and was not—as people say—ready to quit his day job. But he was ready to start his career.

Career Issues

In this story, David faces four career questions:

▮ How much security is he willing to give up to become an actor?

▮ How can he make his interest in acting an income-producing career choice?

▮ If he cannot make a sufficient income in acting, what else can he do as an actor to augment his income?

▮ What other occupations can satisfy him?

Here are some related career issues that many people face:

▮ Finding information about an identified occupation

▮ Uniting identified interests, knowledge, and skills in income-producing work

▮ Finding other outlets for identified interests, knowledge, and skills

▮ Identifying the values that must be met for satisfaction in a job

▮ Realizing a sense of inner harmony between ourselves and our work

Reflections

Consider the population of the United States. Consider a drop of water. Consider snowflakes. Wherever we look, we can see multiplicity and variety and at the same time, patterns that create a sense of wholeness. If we step back and talk about the population of the United States, we draw various conclusions about how many men, women, and children there are, or about average heights and weights, or about the various ethnic groups. Move in closer and you see the beauty of each individual human being. Look at the drop of water and you perceive it as one quickly dissolving whole. Move in closer with a microscope and you see a whole world of living microorganisms. If you step out into a snowstorm, you experience snow. Stick out your tongue, and you can taste an individual snowflake. Harmony is the ability to perceive the patterns made by the parts while appreciating each part for itself.

Harmony is associated with the sixth energy center. This center is located in the middle of your forehead, traditionally the location of the third eye. The sixth chakra is associated with the color purple, a deep mix, or harmony, of blue and red. You can visualize a kaleidoscope as an image of this center. As you look into the kaleidoscope, you see the varied pieces broken by light and mirror into ever-increasing patterns. There it is, harmony again—the parts and the whole.

Harmony is the ability to perceive the patterns made by the parts while appreciating each part for itself.

This variety and harmony was described by the English poet Gerard Manley Hopkins (1962), who wrote: "Glory be to God for dappled things. / For skies of couple-color on a brinded cow, / For rose moles all in stipple upon trout that swim." He celebrated variety and pattern in the two colors of a blue-and-white sky and in a brown-and-white cow. He celebrated the pinkish spots on a fish seen through the water with the sun making patterns on those spots. Later in the same poem, Hopkins thanked God for all trades and the varied tools of workers. American poet Walt Whitman (1926/1867) celebrated the diversity of work and workers when he wrote: "I hear America singing, the varied carols I hear." He then described the sounds of all the occupations he heard throughout the United States.

How can we "hear" the full variety of work open to each of us? How can we find harmony in uniting the parts of ourselves identified through self-analysis (as was done in the previous chapter) and the expression of those parts in work? Great poets, like those we have quoted here, understand the details of life through observation and create patterns using their intuition and their artistic sensibilities. But there are other ways of finding out about variety and creating our personal harmony.

Personal harmony comes from doing work that is needed by the world and is an expression of calling. There are many kinds of work that the world needs. The needed work of the world is not limited to the "helping" professions, nor is it static. It changes with time. If you were living a hundred years ago, all the work that relates to information systems as we know them today would not need doing. The work would not be there because there were insufficient underlying structures. The structures that later came into being included both the development of tech-

Personal harmony comes from doing work that is needed by the world and is an expression of calling.

nology and the development of a community of people with the ideas to support an industry. As another example, Beethoven was able to write the great symphonies because of his gifts, the technology of the instruments that had been developed by his lifetime, and the concept of the community of the orchestra. So the work that needs doing today is the work that is out there to be done, that enhances human life in any way, and that is performed in an ethical manner.

In our story, David is in a state of disharmony. He knows his calling. It's acting. He has known this for more than five years.

He thinks about acting every day, but he does nothing about answering the calling. David has a good job. It is work that enhances the lives of others. It is work that needs doing. And David does his job well and in an ethical manner. But it is not the job for him. He is not happy. He is bored because he has not found the harmony of a good job that corresponds to his calling. Then David gets the message from his unexpected wise person. Shirley Garson bemoans her own lack of action because the time has never seemed right for her. When David hears Shirley, he gets a wake-up call. Before this he was unable to move because he was afraid of losing security. He simply didn't have enough information.

In the last chapter you looked at how to discover your calling. This chapter focuses on how you can uncover the work that needs doing in the world and how to make choices about which part you want to do at a given time. We call this the search for career information. Just as in the last chapter there was a pragmatic aspect to finding your calling, so in this chapter you will look at practical means of finding career information. Some people see practical work as separate from spiritual practices or beliefs. In this book the practical and the spiritual form a whole. There again is the theme of this chapter—harmony.

These are the major sections of this set of reflections:

- Harmony and the Adventure of Searching

- Knowing When to Search for Career Information

- Asking the Right Questions

- Finding Harmony by Searching the World

- Finding Harmony from Within

Harmony and the Adventure of Searching

Adventure suggests action, risk, and the possibility of surprise, the unexpected, even danger. To find harmony between calling and work, one must first undergo the adventure of searching. The quest is for the place between that which is available to you and that which you want to do. So the adventure begins by opening up the wide world of possibilities and ends by narrowing to choice. Adventurers begin their journeys with many paths, turnings in the paths, byways and highways. They do not know what is on these roads because the roads have yet to be traveled. By journey's end, the adventurers not only know where they are, but how they got there.

In myth, the adventure is often called the hero's journey. Joseph Campbell (Campbell & Moyers, 1988) pointed out that some heroes and heroines may undertake the journey deliberately, with a goal in mind. Other heroes and heroines find themselves thrown into adventures. You too may be undertaking the hero's journey by choice or circumstance. You may have identified career disharmony and decided to make a change. Or the change may have been forced upon you by external circumstances. It is natural to feel apprehensive about the journey. It may be helpful to remember that we are born as adventurers. We make the journey from the watery comfort of our mother's womb to the external, unprotected environment. This journey, like every adventure, has both psychological and physical aspects. The importance of this idea was developed by psychologist Otto Rank and utilized by Campbell in his discussion of the hero's journey.

This idea, that we are born adventurers, is particularly important because the adventure of finding work, like birth, is ultimately transforming and has both physical and psychological import. Physical effects can be seen in the relationship between work and how we live, where we live, even with whom we live. The work itself may affect our eating, sleeping, exercising, and recreational patterns. Work that is disharmonious can produce stresses that result in sickness. Similarly, the work we do can alter our psychological responses. We can move from despair to bliss and feel good or bad about ourselves depending on what we do and how we do it. When we move from disharmonious to harmonious work, we can be transformed.

If we refuse to undertake the journey, we refuse to search, and if we do not search, we cannot find the treasure of new information. We limit our sights only to the information about work that we already have. All of us have acquired information about work from people we observe around us, from newspapers, from television comedies and dramas, from movies. It is not that the information we gather casually is incorrect. The problem is that it is insufficient. If you do not go beyond the knowledge that simply comes to you, if you do not go on the hero's journey, you cannot know what is beyond. You cannot know all the variety that is open to you.

David took a job temporarily and was then held by what he described as "velvet claws." That image suggests that he wanted to move but felt he was restrained by external forces, even if those forces were somewhat benign. (They were after all velvet!) But were the forces really external? The forces that kept David in the Rainbow Hotel chain were not external. The first

If you do not go beyond the knowledge that simply comes to you, if you do not go on the hero's journey, you cannot know what is beyond.

was his own internal need for security. Because that need was met, he did not set out on his adventure. The second was his need to please his parents. Because he thought they might not approve of his choice of acting, he did not begin the search. But David had other needs. He needed to exercise his talents. That is why he felt such longing and daydreamed in front of the dollhouses. Instead of beginning the actual journey of searching, he pretended to search.

Many people put off their search or pretend to search. They always have a reason for starting tomorrow. They believe they have begun but they limit their quest for information to sources they have always used. They play, "Yes, but . . ." games. They tell themselves, "I would do it, but nothing will ever change." They stop themselves, not in midstream, but before they have even entered the water above their ankles.

Knowing When to Search for Career Information

David experienced several of the major cues that it was time to search. He was bored with his work. He spent a lot of time daydreaming. He lived for the breaks in work. When his co-worker, Judy, asked him what kind of days he liked, he realized that he didn't like any of his days at work.

David's cues are signals that many people experience. There are other signals as well. One cue is feeling discontented with where you are living although you have been happy living there for some time. Another cue is in your relationships with other people. You may find yourself losing your temper with co-workers, customers, or family members over minor issues or issues that would not have bothered you in the past. You may find that you crave sleep although you have gotten enough rest. On the other hand, you may find yourself restless and unable to sleep at night. Changes in health habits, particularly overeating and underexercising as compared to your usual patterns, can signal disharmony in work. Of course, other kinds of stress—including physical illness—can have related symptoms, and you must identify the source for yourself. If the source is disharmony in work, it's time to begin the adventure of the search.

Many people encounter life events that seem to suggest it is time for a change. The one with which we are almost all familiar is the transition from full-time student to full-time worker. From the time children are in elementary school, people ask them, "What will you do when you grow up?" As high school and college educations are completed, the pressure is on to make a choice. Some few people know their choices from early years and stay with them. Most people do not make a choice until they are out of school. That time for a lot of people (and their parents) is a time of panic. Choice is often made with insufficient career information. The hero's journey is avoided for the time being.

Another common time for career dissatisfaction is at the time one's children leave home. The famous "empty-nest syndrome" occurs not only for women but for men. So much time, energy, and other resources have been focused on the family. Now those needs are reduced. And the empty-nester parent finds time for self-examination. This is another time for some people to begin the adventure. Divorce, separation, death of a partner may also spark the psychological or economic need for searching.

Still other people who appear to be settled in midcareer are really ready to begin the journey again. They may be at the top

The famous "empty-nest syndrome" occurs not only for women but for men.

of their aspirations within a particular occupation, such as vice president of sales for a major corporation, but they are no longer experiencing harmony between their calling and their work. They may be silently asking themselves, "Is that all there is?" There are also people who recognize that they will never make it to what they define as the top. They may be asking, "Is there some other place for me?"

Another group of people who need to search are people preparing for retirement. The age of retirement is now a choice for many people. Some people choose to leave long-standing

The hero's journey may be undertaken at any age and more than once.

jobs earlier so that they can seek other work that will be more sat-isfying in some way. And it is not unusual for those who retire at more traditional ages to want new work experiences. The hero's journey may be undertaken at any age and more than once.

In our story, David had left school with incomplete and erro-neous career information. He believed that he could gain satis-faction in his calling by "acting" the part of the genial hotel clerk. However, he had not really explored the duties of the hotel clerk and the repetitious nature of the job. He didn't real-ize how much this would bore him, and how often he would have to retreat to the dollhouse. In addition, he did not seem to have explored any other career options.

For many people, there are particular periods in life when they are more likely to experience discontent at work even if they have been happy up to that point. During the transition from one major stage of life to another, you are likely to experience disruptions in career and spirituality.

Successful accomplishment of the transition depends on successful completion of the tasks and challenges of the previous stage. Erik Erikson (1963) defined eight stages of life, each with its own task. In each stage the task is to resolve a conflict between opposing outcomes. We must remember that these stages are generalizations based on Erikson's observations of people in industrialized Western societies. Everyone does not experience the same degree of struggle in each stage. Nor does everyone experience the stages at the precise ages identified by Erikson. Use the following information to consider transitions you may have faced in the past, may be experiencing now, or may face in the future. The eight stages are:

- Stage 1: Trust vs. mistrust (birth to 18 months)—If trust is achieved, the outcome is hope.

- Stage 2: Autonomy vs. shame and doubt (18 months to 3 years)—If autonomy is achieved, the outcome is will.

- Stage 3: Initiative vs. guilt (3 to 6 years)—If initiative is achieved, the outcome is purpose.

- Stage 4: Industry vs. inferiority (6 to 12 years)—If industry is achieved, the outcome is competence.

- Stage 5: Identity vs. role confusion (12 to 20 years)—If identity is achieved, the outcome is fidelity to self.

- Stage 6: Intimacy vs. isolation (20 to 35 years)—If intimacy is achieved, the outcome is love.

- Stage 7: Generativity vs. stagnation (35 years to retirement)—If generativity is achieved, the outcome is care.

- Stage 8: Integrity vs. despair (retirement years)—If integrity is achieved, the outcome is wisdom.

Each stage or period of transition may demand of you another search for work that implements your calling and leads to harmony. The work sought by the young adult whose life is centered on finding a mate and having a family is likely to be different from the work that same person, with the same calling, will find harmonious when he or she is in middle or late adulthood. Carolyn Heilbrun (1988), who is also known as the mystery writer Amanda Cross, makes the point that for many generations women often have not found their calling and could not begin the work that has meaning in the world until they were in their

> *Before you can get a clear answer, you must ask a clear question.*

middle years, their fifties. As the workplace continues to change for women, their stages and work patterns may become more like those of men. However, women continue to be the bearers of children and so some stages of career development may remain different from those of men. On the other hand, as men take on additional home responsibilities, their career stages may differ from those traditionally identified. Only you can assess your own life circumstances and know when it is time to begin or repeat your adventure. Remember, you will probably search for career information several times in your lifetime.

Asking the Right Questions

Before you can get a clear answer, you must ask a clear question. In our story, David never asked clear questions about the opportunities he might have in the theater. Instead he daydreamed about an unrealizable future. This part of the reflections is about the kinds of questions you may want to ask about any job or occupation. These questions fall under the general heading of *career information*. Career information includes all the knowledge about the external world that you need to make informed decisions about occupations, organizations that you are considering as possible places of work, and about specific jobs. An occupation is the more general description of a field of work. For example, banker, butcher, belly dancer, and boat salesperson are all occupations. A job is the combination of an occupation and an organization. For example, teller at Citibank, meat cutter at Safeway, belly dancer at the Oriental Oasis, and salesperson for Sail Away Boats are all jobs.

The following topics are the elements of occupational information that most people find important. The topics are listed in descending order of importance.

- Description of the occupation

- Education and training required

- Job duties

- Entry-level skills required

- Occupational outlook

- Earnings and benefits

- Industries in which the occupation is found

- Interests of workers in the field

- Abilities of workers in the field

- Licensing and certification requirements

- Related occupations

- Environmental and working conditions

- Career ladders

- Supply and demand of workers

There are a number of factors that are generally related to job satisfaction. These factors are most often associated with particular organizations rather than with occupations or individual jobs within the organization. You will find that some of these elements of job satisfaction are more important to you than others. Remember that part of finding your calling is related to identifying your values. This is a point at which your internal and external requirements must harmonize. You may recognize that some of the following elements are also elements of information about individual jobs. However, in many organizations, the culture is strong and the information will be similar across jobs. Do not worry if you use items listed in one category to ask questions about one of the other categories. The important thing to do is to use the items to develop your own list of questions about the information of worth to you.

- Recognition of your worth by your supervisor and others

- Opportunities for achievement

- Possibility for growth

- Chance for advancement

- Interpersonal relations with your co-workers and others

- Ability of supervisors to judge your work fairly and help you perform better

- Supervisory consideration of you as a human being

- Opportunity to participate in decision making

- Policy and administration of the organization as a whole

- Physical working conditions such as lighting and ventilation

- Effect of hours of work and travel on your personal life

- Status of the organization and your role within it

- Job security within the organization and of the organization itself

- Potential growth of the organization

- Ability of the organization to adapt quickly to changes

- Encouragement of individuality and diversity

- Respect for employees as peers and self-managers

The final list of items includes information you may want to have before deciding to accept a particular job offer. Again, your task is to choose the items of importance to you.

- Major job responsibilities
- Freedom to carry out the job in ways that work best
- Use of skills, knowledge, and abilities in carrying out work
- Projects I will carry out
- Why others left this job
- My immediate supervisor
- Hours of work
- The nature of the people the organization serves
- Vacation policy
- Sick-leave policy
- Starting salary
- Salary increases
- Health insurance and other benefits
- Educational benefits
- Stock options or other incentives

When you are carrying out your search for career information, there are questions you must ask yourself to give meaning to the information you find. Perhaps the most important area of self-questioning centers around setting. Aspects of setting you might want to consider include any of the following:

- In what part of the world you want to live
- What kind of area (urban, rural, small town) you prefer
- How far you are willing to travel to work
- How far you are willing to relocate
- Your preferred size of organization
- Your preference for working in the public or private sector

However, for all the categories and specifics of information you gather, the information is meaningless until you measure it against your own needs and desires. Even the questions about salary have no meaning until you consider the compensation that you believe is fair for the job, appropriate to your needs, and satisfying to your ego.

When you are carrying out your search for career information, there are questions you must ask yourself to give meaning to the information you find.

Finding Harmony by Searching the World

Career information is everywhere. Some career information is organized into books, stand-alone computer systems, or sites on the World Wide Web. Other information requires more work on your part because it is not presented as career information, although it is equally valuable.

Let's look at the more organized information first. Your local library is an excellent source of printed information. In the library, you can find individual books about occupations or industries. You can also find a print edition of the major source of information about all occupations, the *Occupational Outlook Handbook* (OOH, 1998). The OOH has been published by the Bureau of Labor Statistics of the U.S. Department of Labor since 1949. It provides descriptions of approximately 250 occupations including working conditions, qualifications, and outlook for the future. The occupations included in the OOH include almost all of the occupations available in the United States as well as in most other industrialized countries.

In addition to information from the federal government, in the United States each state has an organization equivalent to the Department of Labor and a State Occupational Information Coordinating Committee. These state organizations publish information ranging from pamphlets to newspapers that contain valuable material on local labor market trends and opportunities.

In business libraries, you will also have access to annual corporate reports that may prove useful if a corporation is the setting in which you wish to work.

In libraries, schools, and some other locations, you also may have access to computerized career-information delivery systems. These systems generally include the kind of occupational information we discussed in the last section of these reflections. In addition, they usually include information about educational programs and institutions. Some systems link the educational information to the occupational information showing which programs prepare people for particular occupations. The systems often go beyond simply providing information and help individuals facilitate the processes of linking external information with self-information.

If you have access to the World Wide Web or the Internet, you can also find information about jobs, organizations, résumé writing, and online job fairs. You can even find a job listing, get information about the job, apply for the job by sending your résumé electronically, and get interviewed and hired without ever leaving your home computer. Techniques for doing this are described in Deborah Bloch's *How to Write a Winning Resume,* fourth edition, and *How to Have a Winning Interview,* third edition. If you have any experience using the Internet, you know that Web sites come and go too quickly to be reliably reported in any detail in this book. However, two sites that have had longevity and may prove of continuing use are www.careermosaic.com and http://stats.bls.gov./ocohome.htm. The first is a privately run career resource center with many links within it. The second is the home page for the OOH. While the print and on-line versions contain the same information, the on-line version allows you to search the information by key word, by index, and by job cluster. You may want to look for books about searching for occupational information on the Internet in your local library or bookstore.

The sources we have discussed thus far organize career information for the reader. However, other print sources carry information about the world of work that is important if you want to stay abreast of trends in any field. Your local newspaper, the *Wall Street Journal*, news magazines, and the business, science, arts, leisure, and news sections of major newspapers such as the *New York Times* may all have information that will be pertinent to you in your search. You can stay up to date in a general way by broad, regular reading. You can also use the indexes of these various publications to search for specific information about occupations, developments in a field, or even organizations.

Don't forget people. Remember to find people who are in similar positions to those that interest you, talk to people in the organizations you are considering, and learn about industries by attending meetings of people in similar fields.

David was in dire need of information. All he knew about was how to get further education. And he got that information from a former teacher. He did not have any information about occupational options open to him in the field of acting. Nor did he know anything about related fields. He could have used both the formally organized and the informal sources of career information to increase his sense of harmony. From formal sources he

You turn information into knowledge by giving it a pattern or by adding it to a pattern or framework you already hold in your mind.

could have learned of occupations related to the theater other than acting. If he didn't succeed in supporting himself as an actor, these might have been more satisfactory to him than the hotel job. From informal sources such as other actors, he might also have found where there were opportunities for part-time or temporary work that could be used to support himself as he tried to make an acting career.

In all you do, remember that the purpose of your quest, your adventure, your search is to find the work that needs doing and through which you can express your calling. Remember that harmony exists in finding patterns in the variety of information.

You turn information into knowledge by giving it a pattern or by adding it to a pattern or framework you already hold in your mind. The outline for the ways to acquire information that we have provided is general. Only you can give it the specifics that inspirit the information and inspire you.

Finding Harmony from Within

The search processes described above require activity of one sort. There is another sort of activity that can also produce harmony. It is the practice of mindfulness, meditation, or stillness. Stillness is difficult to practice. It requires the discipline of doing nothing in a life that is otherwise filled with action. Meditation is practiced in many cultures and traditions. Among the aboriginal people of Australia there is a practice called *dadirri*. Dadirri is described as an inner deep listening, a quiet stillness that makes people feel whole and renews them. This description of dadirri is echoed in the beautiful set of directions for meditation given by Krishnamurti (1992/1958): "Sit very quietly and be still not only physically, not only in your body, but also in your mind. Be very still and then in that stillness, attend. Attend to the sounds outside this building, the cock crowing, the birds, somebody coughing, somebody leaving. Listen first to the things outside you, then listen to what is going on in your mind. And you will then see, if you listen very, very attentively, in that silence, that the outside sound and the inside sound are the same."

When stillness is practiced, harmonious order is recognized. Krishnamurti described the harmony of the seekers with the world outside themselves—"the outside sound and the inside sound are the same." In the practice of stillness, answers to asked and unasked questions often become clear to the person meditating. A sense of the order of the universe may come to you if you meditate. And with this sense of order comes a sense of meaningfulness in one's life or a sense of where meaning can come from. Mindfulness is a way of knowing that comes from quiet self-examination without thinking.

In our story, David spends a lot of time daydreaming. Do not confuse daydreaming with meditation. In meditation there is an active desire to quiet the mind and observe that which passes through it without external stimulation. Daydreaming has its place, but it is not the same as meditation.

You have practiced a form of meditation in the applications for each chapter. This is a meditation in which you relax your body, quiet your mind, and then deliberately use the relaxed

Mindfulness is a way of knowing that comes from quiet self-examination without thinking.

state for guided visualization and affirmations. Again, these are worthwhile activities but they are different from mindfulness meditation. In mindfulness meditation, you put no thoughts in your mind. You seek stillness by simply observing the thoughts that pass your way.

Through meditation, the harmony that you are seeking between your internal search for self-information and your external search for career information will come to you. Through meditation, you will experience the harmony of the hero's journey and your calling.

Harmony and Spirituality — Some Concluding Thoughts

Many people are shackled to jobs, whether they call the bonds "velvet claws" as David did or "golden handcuffs." Some of these people stay in place for a lifetime, longing for their retirements when they are decades away from them. These people never really live. They never exercise their calling or find their harmony.

Just as David got a wake-up call from his wise person, Shirley Garson, so you may get a wake-up call from an unexpected source. Surely, you do not want to be one of the shackled people. There are many ways to break the bonds. You may find another job to take the place of the one you have. Or you may take advantage of the part-time opportunities of the economy to find your harmony. One person we know, Barry, was a very successful marketing executive with a Fortune 500 company. He was so stressed by the mismatch between his calling and his job that his physical symptoms caused him to go on disability. During the disability period, he discovered a passion for baking. In addition, to relax himself he began to get massages. He found the massages so helpful that he decided to study massage and open a practice. Meanwhile, he continued to bake in his spare time and to give his confections to his friends. Fortunately the disability period ended. His health stabilized. But he did not return to his job. He now earns his living baking, giving massages, and when economic circumstances make it necessary, he takes temporary data processing jobs in his old company. Barry always knew his job did not satisfy any of his gifts or interests, but he made a lot of money. He remained gripped in the velvet claws until, forced by the circumstance of illness, he had to take the hero's journey.

If you are missing harmony now, begin the hero's journey today. If you feel you are in harmony, gather information, know the sources, so that when circumstances around you change or you change with age, you are ready to take the hero's journey. In your mental closet, keep your backpack of information-seeking tools polished and ready. You, the hero, the heroine, are always ready for life's adventure.

Applications

In this chapter we looked at how we can develop harmony by investigating and understanding the variety of opportunities that will meet our interests, abilities, skills, knowledge, and values. The applications that follow are designed to help you in four ways:

- To see more clearly the work that you think needs doing in the world

- To identify the career information questions of greatest importance to you

- To find information about at least one occupation, organization, or job of potential interest to you

- To experience the harmony of answering your calling

Application 1: In the Dollhouse

This exercise will help you see the kind of work you believe needs doing in the world. In our story, David daydreamed about acting whenever he was near the dollhouses, but he did not know the importance of his daydreams. Actually they told him the work that needed doing in the world and his relation to it. In this exercise, you will daydream deliberately.

Directions: In your mind, create a dollhouse that is a miniature work setting of some kind. Visualize yourself inside the setting. Give yourself a name. You may use a name you make up, a name from fiction, or the name of a real person, living or dead. Allow yourself to roam around the dollhouse. Observe yourself. How are you dressed? Are you wearing any special kind of uniform or work clothes? What are you holding? What are you doing? Who else is there? What relationship do you have to anyone else who is there? Stay in the dollhouse as long as you'd like, and when you come out answer the following questions.

In the Dollhouse

1. What did the setting of the dollhouse tell you about the kind of workplace you would enjoy?

2. Think about the name you gave yourself. What does it suggest about the kind of role you like to play at work or in life?

3. What did your clothes reveal about the kind of work you were doing in your imagination?

4. What did the objects you held or touched show you about the kind of work you were doing in your imagination?

5. How did you relate to the people in your imagination? What does it suggest to you about the work you would like to do?

6. Look over your answers to the first five questions. What clues are there in your daydreams about work you believe needs doing in the world?

7. If you are interested in beginning the journey to that work, what first steps will you take?

Application 2: Ask a Clear Question

In the chapter, you saw many topics for questions that you might ask about an occupation, organization, or job. In this exercise, you will clarify the questions that are of greatest importance to you.

Directions: Look over the lists of topics of career information. Choose five to seven topics from each category, and write the questions you would like answered in the space below.

Ask a Clear Question

Questions About Occupations

1.

2.

3

4.

5.

Questions About Organizations

1.

2.

3.

4.

5.

Questions About Jobs

1.

2.

3.

4.

5.

Application 3: Get a Clear Answer

This exercise is designed to help you practice the skills of information gathering from formal and informal sources.

Directions: Identify an occupation, organization, and (if possible) a job that interest you. Use as many sources of information as possible to get the answers to the questions you identified as important in Application 2. In addition to writing the information in the spaces provided, after each answer, write the source of the information.

Get a Clear Answer

Answers About the Occupation of _____

1.

Source of information:

2.

Source of information:

3.

Source of information:

4.

Source of information:

5.

Source of information:

Answers About the Organization Named _____

1.

Source of information:

2.

Source of information:

3.

Source of information:

4.

Source of information:

5.

Source of information:

Answers About the Job of _____

1.

Source of information:

2.

Source of information:

3.

Source of information:

4.

Source of information:

5.

Source of information:

Application 4: A Meditation on Harmony

Directions: You may want to ask someone else to read this slowly to you, or you may want to read the meditation into a tape recorder for yourself before you begin. This meditation begins like all the others with directions that will put you in a receptive frame of mind and spirit.

Sit in a comfortable chair with a firm back, or on the floor with your back straight and your legs crossed comfortably. Place your hands on your thighs, palms up and slightly open. Straighten yourself as if you were about to pay attention. Now let your shoulders drop naturally. Breathe slowly in through your nose and out through your mouth. You may make a sound with your breath as you exhale. That's fine. Just breathe in and out deeply and evenly for a few moments. Let your breath return to normal.

Begin to feel the power of the earth wherever your body is in contact with the floor or chair. Maintain your contact with the abundant power of the physical, material world. Let the energy of the brown and red earth, its dryness, its moist fertility enter your body. Keep the earth's energy within you. At the same time, become aware of the top of your head. Imagine you can feel the electricity of all the spirit in the cosmos. As you draw in one breath, draw in the abundance of the earth. Exhale. As you draw in the next breath, draw in the light of the cosmos. Picture this as you breathe in and out. Any time you lose your concentration in the exercise, just return to your breathing.

Move your attention to the first energy center, the one at the base of your spine. See the red disk spinning at that energy center. Breathe in and out of the red disk several times.

Now move your attention to your pelvis. Picture an orange disk spinning around your pelvis. This is the energy of your second energy center. Breathe into the orange disk.

Move your attention to the third energy center at your midsection. See the yellow disk spinning at that energy center. Breathe in and out of the yellow disk.

Now focus your attention on the middle of your chest, at your heart. See the green disk of this energy center. Spin the green disk with your breath.

Focus your attention on your throat. Picture the blue disk spinning at your throat. Breathe in and out of the blue disk. Keep the blue disk spinning.

Now slowly move your attention to the middle of your forehead. This is the energy center of your third eye, the energy center of intuition. Picture a purple disk spinning at this energy center. Breathe in and out of the purple disk. Breathe purple down your body and legs right to your toes. Breathe purple out to the edges of your fingertips. Keep breathing in and out of the purple disk. Picture a kaleidoscope held to your third eye at the center of your forehead. As you look into the kaleidoscope you see the beautiful fragments of colored glass as they form one elaborate pattern after another. Spin the kaleidoscope with the purple breathing energy. See the harmony of the glass fragments. See the patterns and exult in their beauty. Keep the kaleidoscope in view as long as you'd like. Slowly let the kaleidoscope become a purple disk once more and keep breathing in and out of it for a few more moments.

Keep your eyes closed and repeat the following affirmations four times.

I see the work that needs doing.
I can do the work that needs doing.
I am in harmony with the world.

When you are ready, slowly open your eyes.

Application 5: In Your Own Voice—Continuing Your Journal

Continue your journal by noting your thoughts on the story of David. Consider the reflections that follow the story. What questions or ideas did they raise for your own use? Did you feel challenged to begin the adventure? What other feelings did you have about the idea of the quest? How close to (or far from) your own harmony do you feel? Keep writing in your journal and rereading it.

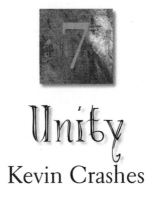

Unity

Kevin Crashes

The Story

Kevin clicked on his e-mail icon and settled down to read the latest from work. He could hear his wife in the background taking care of their newborn baby girl, and the combination of the hum of his latest computer mingled with the timeless sounds of baby care filled him with delight. He was glad he had taken the ninety days of paternity leave and, even now, after the three months, he was reluctant to return to the office. He liked his job as a software engineer, but wished he could always work from home.

The mailbox flashed its usual morning message, "You have new mail." "OK," he clicked back and began to scan the list. What was his buddy, Micky, sending with the subject line containing just one word "One . . ."? Kev opened the message. The rest of it read, "for the money, two for the show—get ready for some fireworks and get your butt down here fast!"

Kevin packed up his gear, kissed Lizzie and the baby goodbye, and headed down to his office in what he thought of as Tech Town.

"What's the bottom line?" he asked Micky.

Micky looked uncomfortable as he answered, "It's finally happened. Downsizing has hit our little world. I guess that failure to meet last quarter's projections really hit deeper than we thought. Listen, why don't you go to your office and . . ."

Kevin could see Micky's discomfort, so he headed for his own space, hardly an office, just one more cubicle in the feeding trough of software production. A note asking him to see his boss was propped up against his monitor. Kevin knew what the note meant. He was one of those who would now be "outplaced." He had seen this happen to friends in other companies, but he never thought it would happen here or to him. Of course, that was why Micky was squirming. There was no privacy in the world of open office systems.

After Kevin had gotten the official news, he picked up his backpack and left for home. He would have plenty of time to deal with all the routines they had waiting for him. And they certainly couldn't fire him for leaving early.

He knew that Lizzie would see that something was wrong as soon as she saw him, so he made no effort to hide his feelings as he came in the door. Luckily the baby was sleeping and they had some time to talk.

"I'm so mad. I could spit bullets. After all the work I gave them, the ideas, the shape of so many programs, the applications. I just can't believe they would do this to me. Even in the last three months, I've made myself available for questions on the projects I was working on, and you know how they took advantage of what was supposed to be 'my time.' They weren't even paying me and I worked for them."

Lizzie heard him out and knew he had to talk about his feelings. However, she also knew the baby would wake up any minute, and she didn't want to leave him just feeling sorry for himself. She was upset too, but she thought maybe she could just calm him down a little.

"Listen," she said, "those jerks! You gave so much to the start-up of the company. How could they let you go? Just three months ago they wanted to make you the manager of a new group. And thank goodness this has come after you were able to exercise your options from the startup of the company. We've really gotten our house payments down to a minimum. And listen—I hear Patty beginning to cry—what about your idea that you want to be a consultant? Do you think you could get that off the ground before we are in real trouble?" And Lizzie went to get the baby.

Kevin put his head in his hands. He knew she was trying to comfort him, but he wasn't satisfied. For the first time he actually felt jealous of his own kid. "This makes me feel even worse," he thought. "Not only will I fail as the famous 'breadwinner,' but I'm turning into one of those jerks who can't decide if he's a father or another baby."

"Lizzie," he called, "I've got to walk some of this off. I'll be back before Patty's bedtime bottle. Call me at Ping's if you need me before then."

Ping was an unlikely friend. She was quite a bit older than Kevin and Lizzie, but not quite old enough to be a substitute mom. Kevin had met Ping when he was in the library book club, and although they seemed to have little in common on the surface, they both liked the same books. And they both detested the book club leader, whom they found to be a pompous know-nothing. Coffees after the library discussion had turned into meals at each others' homes and a real friendship for all. Ping was even Patty's godmother.

All the way to Ping's, and it was a long walk, Kevin rehearsed telling her his bad news. But all he could say when he walked in was, "Shit, I've been fired."

Ping sat him down, made some tea, and listened as he went from anger to sadness and back to anger. She waited for him to get to the idea she knew he had been toying with even before this happened. She knew he wanted to break away from the corporate life and be on his own as a consultant, but up to this point, he hadn't really been ready to give up the security of the job and its steady, substantial salary. Finally, she asked, "So what next? Where to now, software soldier?"

"If only I were like you," he answered. "You always seem to have it together, while I always feel pulled apart."

Ping raised her eyebrows in surprise. "Always have it together? Let me tell you my little tale. When I was fresh out of college, I had a teaching certificate in hand, but no job. I was on a waiting list for teachers, but needed a job right away. I took the postal service exam and got a job. That's how it all began. First I was a mail handler and moved mail from one place to another. After a half year of the shift work handling mail, I took another test, and got promoted to letter sorter. Then, a teaching offer came, but my pay in the post office put me way beyond the salary for a starting teacher. I felt caught in golden handcuffs. I wanted to teach but needed the overtime money I could earn. I was helping my mom too at that time. I stayed as a letter sorter for eleven years. I was making good money but felt really dissatisfied with myself. I knew I was smarter than the job needed."

Kevin actually forgot about himself as he listened to Ping. "Eleven years," he repeated. "I never knew about that. I thought you were always in the white-collar part of the post office. Don't you do management training?"

"Now I do, but it took me a long time to get there. I applied for lots of promotions and lots of jobs. After a lot of lousy breaks, I finally gave up. I figured they were paying for my boredom. Then the unexpected happened. The postal service was trying to catch up with the rest of the world and brought in someone to see why some workers were so dissatisfied. The service was worried about its bad press. So this guy came around. He was a typical postal service kind of guy. A buttoned-up manager with a military air. He got some groups together. Focus groups to focus on how people worked in teams, and how they could change their work patterns. I had seniority and security, and figured, 'what the hell!' When he asked questions about the work, I answered up! So that's how my new career began. He invited me to be part of a new training group that would change some postal service operations—and the rest is history."

Kevin shook his head. "I don't think Lizzie would be very happy if I took eleven years to make my next move."

Ping smiled and said, "It took me a long time to get it all together."

Career Issues

In this story, Kevin asked himself four questions:

▪ How was he going to support his family without the corporate job he had held?

▪ How could he take advantage of the momentary freedom offered by the downsizing?

▪ How could he get his life together so that he felt as good about what he was doing as Ping felt about her life?

▪ How could he earn the living he needed and have time for his young family?

Here are some related career issues that many people face:

▪ Fear of losing a job and all that goes with the job

▪ Letting go of a job in which we have invested a great deal of self

▪ Developing a support system for career growth

▪ Getting it all together

▪ Keeping it together when circumstances pull at the edges

▪ Trusting in the abundance of the universe

Reflections

This is a story about having to pull it all together—and recognizing that you can never achieve this completely. As soon as you pull it all together, something else starts to change. This is true no matter what the *it* is for you. You may think your job is secure and you have all your finances planned for the next decade.

The paradox is that even when things seem most together,
they are coming apart. And even as things seem to come apart,
since they are all part of a whole, they are really together.

Then along comes an unexpected need for funds, inflation, a change in your organization's policies, or an inheritance. What you thought you had all figured out no longer computes! You may think you have completed your education and you will never study again. Then along comes a new technology at work and you have to master it. Or you read a book that captures your imagination and sets you off in a new direction of learning. This chapter is about unity, and unity incorporates a paradox. The paradox is that even when things seem most together, they are coming apart. And even as things seem to come apart, since they are all part of a whole, they are really together.

The trick in life is to believe in unity and, because of this belief, to trust the universe. Trusting the universe does not mean being unprepared for life's changes. It includes both being prepared for changes and understanding that your preparations may be needed in unanticipated ways. This belief in unity is the essence of spirituality. One.

The sense of oneness is centered in the crown chakra, the energy center at the top of your head. Picture rays of white light emanating from the top of your head reaching higher and higher until they are out of sight and filling the entire universe. This is the essence of unity, and the sound of unity is *Om*. Try it, and you will find your whole body vibrating to the music of the spheres.

In Judaism a central prayer begins, "Hear, O Israel, the Lord our God, the Lord is One." Some Jewish people believe that this prayer was written to help the early Jews distinguish themselves from people of other religions who believed in many gods. However, we believe that it has a meaning beyond that interpretation. The meaning is that God equals One. The experience of spirituality is the experience of connectedness to everything, and that is the experience of God. That is our interpretation of the prayer, and our interpretation of all spiritual quests. We also see this interpretation in Christianity. The worship of the Trinity, the Father, the Son, and the Holy Spirit is also the worship of One.

The transcendent moment is the moment when you feel the sense of union with something that is at the same time higher than yourself and your deepest self.

This is known as a Mystery: three Persons, one God. Similarly in Eastern religions, the many aspects of God, although depicted separately, are all aspects of the One.

Unity is the goal of all religious practice. The transcendent moment is the moment when you feel the sense of union with something that is at the same time higher than yourself and your deepest self. Great mystics of all faiths—Teresa of Avila, Buddha, Mohammed, and Moses—experience the transcendent, the sense of One, more than most other people. In the introduction to the *Power of Myth* (Campbell & Moyers, 1988), Bill Moyers tells a story of the Indian saint Ramakrishna and a woman who came to him. The woman told Ramakrishna that she could not love God. Ramakrishna asked her if there was anything she loved. She replied that she loved her little nephew. Ramakrishna then said to her, "There is your love and service to God in your love and service to that little child." Why is this so? How is the love of one's child also the love of God? Because they are One.

The truth of One is found in all religions and in myths and stories throughout the ages. Unity, oneness, was also taught by

Jesus when he told his followers, "What you do to the least of my brothers, you do also to me." Poet John Donne (1952/1624) reminded us that "No man is an island entire of itself. . . . So do not ask for whom the bell tolls, it tolls for thee." And in the *Star Wars* films, the hero, Luke Skywalker, acquires a sense of truth from the wise one, Obeonekenobe, or O-be-one. This sense of oneness also means being true to yourself. That is what Luke Skywalker learns.

The importance of oneness to the human psyche has been stressed in psychology as well as in religion. Psychologists call this recognition of unity a "peak experience." The peak experience has been described as the highest level of human awareness by psychologists from William James (1902) and Carl Jung (1971/1953) to Abraham Maslow (1968) and Carl Rogers (1961). On the other hand, psychologists have also recognized the

It takes time to achieve a sense of fulfillment and to recognize what has been there all the time in the universe.

importance of developing our individuality. In Chapter 6, we looked at the stages of development described by Erikson. The most critical stage, according to Erikson, is the development of identity, our individuality. We can say that individuality is the path to the goal of unity.

Our story begins when Kevin believes that things are falling apart. He believes that Ping has everything held together and has always had a life that is perfect in this way. From Ping, Kevin learns that unity in life is hard-won. It takes time to achieve a sense of fulfillment and to recognize what has been there all the time in the universe. One woman we know was shopping for a house in a city new to her. The real estate agent took her to many properties over a several-month period. Each time, something was not quite right. Either the house was missing some feature essential to the woman, she made an offer too late in the process, or her offer was too low. This was, as the agent said, "a hot market." The woman began to despair and expressed her feelings to the agent. "You really shouldn't worry," he said. "Remember, the house you are going to buy is already there. We just have to find it." And, of course, they did.

Since we cannot hold *it*, the reflections in this chapter are all about letting go and finding *it*. The sections of the reflections are:

▪ Unity of Career

▪ Unity with Others

▪ Unity of Energy

▪ Unity of Spirit

Unity of Career

To understand the unity of your career, it is important that you remember the work you did on calling. Your calling is the combination of all of your gifts—interests, skills, knowledge, personality characteristics, and values. You live these gifts in all of your life, not in just one job. Remember all of the roles you play in your life. You can define your career narrowly in terms of work you do for pay. Or you can define your career to include all of your life work. Your life work includes all you do as a family member, citizen, volunteer, student, and friend. Your life work also includes any activities you participate in by yourself for your own enjoyment, your hobbies or leisure pursuits. Therefore, even when you are out of a job or not working for pay, you are not out of your career as long as you act on your calling. Sometimes you are acutely aware of drawing upon particular gifts. But most of the time, you simply *do*. You don't examine how you are able to *do*.

This brings us back to the examination of another idea we discussed earlier. That is the concept of flow. Flow is the sense of being so absorbed in your work that you have the feeling that you and work are one. You are completely unselfconscious at those moments. It is ironic that when you are most heavily invested in using your gifts, you are least aware of them. But, isn't that what we mean by unity? It is the same paradox as the seeming contradiction of the one in many and the many in one.

In our story, Kevin clearly experienced flow in his job. That is why he was more than willing to work for the company when he was on unpaid paternity leave. It seemed that he feared he would not continue to experience flow once he was forced to leave the job. Kevin makes the mistake many of us make. He believes that the flow comes from the job rather than from him. And that is why he feels so devastated and angry. He is angry that the company is going to deprive him of the harmony of unity between his calling and his work. And that is what he means when he moans to Ping, "If only I were like you. You always seem to have it together, while I feel pulled apart."

When Kevin says that he "*always* feels pulled apart," he is exaggerating. Only that morning, he was "filled with delight" when he was working at his computer and heard his wife and daughter in the background. Now he feels that nothing he does is good enough. That sense of all or nothing is one many of us experience. When some people have reverses at work, it may seem to them that everything is wrong. Instead of feeling the unity of all that is good, they cast a gray shadow over everything they can see. It is as if they want to unify the problems or bad things in their lives.

When people are so wrapped up in the negative, it is hard to begin the hero's journey once again. But that is what must take place sooner or later. The hero's journey is the continuing search for the work that needs doing, the work that is meaningful to each person. One way to look at this is to see yourself as walking your dreamtime path. The dreamtime paths are the routes followed by the Australian aborigines when they go on "walkabouts." These walkabouts are spiritual journeys in which ancestral sites are visited. By taking the walkabout, individuals are put in touch with themselves and their histories. But most important, the walkabout is a period of spiritual growth. You might want to think of your movement down your career path as a walkabout. You examine your self. You search for the work that needs doing. And you synthesize "self" and "search" in the actions you take and the meaning you derive from those actions. Like the aborigines, who must go on walkabouts many times in their lives, you too are always on the spiritual path of self, search, and synthesis in your quest for career unity.

We have tried to communicate that the fear and tension that often accompany job loss and job search are not necessary or productive. Think of yourself as going on a walkabout rather than tell yourself, "I have to get a job." Fear and self-loathing do not produce quicker job-hunting results. One of the least helpful things you can do is to give yourself commands or to verbalize gloom-and-doom results. Many people seem conditioned to predict the worst possible outcome for any setback. They say to themselves, "I can't stand it." "I'll never get a good job." "I'm no

Like the aborigines, who must go on walkabouts many times in their lives, you too are always on the spiritual path of self, search, and synthesis in your quest for career unity

good." "I won't make it." These comments do not produce any result other than increased tension. They increase tension because they separate you from the sense of unity. With every negative description of yourself, you place yourself further from the One. You make yourself feel unworthy of connection. Of course, there is no way you can truly separate yourself since all

Fear and self-loathing do not produce quicker job-hunting results.

of One is One. But you can make yourself feel separate. If you find, in any situation, that you are "dissing" yourself, putting yourself down, insulting yourself—change what you are saying. Instead of saying, "I'll never get a good job. I'm no good." Tell yourself, "It may take some time to find the perfect job for me. I know it's out there, and I'm worth the time it takes."

Unity with Others

In our story, Kevin made two good moves right away. He did not hide the events or his feelings from his wife, Lizzie, and he sought out his friend Ping. Both offered support. His wife, Lizzie, listened. She heard him out as he knew she would. She also empathized with him. She understood his feelings and let him know she did. She also suggested that he remember his own idea of becoming a consultant. Ping was helpful in a different way. She also heard him out. But she confronted him and

When we experience change of any kind, whether it is loss or gain, we need the support of other people. We need some people who will just listen and some people who will help us confront our ideas.

defused his tension and anger when she refused to accept his analysis that only he had problems.

When we experience change of any kind, whether it is loss or gain, we need the support of other people. We need some people who will just listen and some people who will help us confront our ideas. For each of us there is at least one wise person if only we listen hard enough. Allison's change was sparked by the teenager on the bus. Helen's wise person was her son. Bob got his message from the salesman. Perhaps Beatrice's message came from the most unexpected source, a dying man lying in his own wastes. Words of wisdom came to Manny from his wife. That was unexpected because Manny usually got only criticism from her. David's message came from a chance meeting with a hotel guest he would never see again. And in this story, Ping is Kevin's wise person.

If you think about your own life, you may recognize messages that were brought to you by unlikely messengers. This is what the universe provides in its perfect unity. This is part of the universe working for you. The message is already there; we need the ears to listen. Of course, it is difficult to hear messages if we listen to no one.

The more people we know and support, the more people there are to support us when we are in need. This is not a game in which points are scored. It just seems to work that people who help others get help when they need it. They rarely get it from the same people they helped. They simply seem to be part of a giant circle of helpers and the helped. This is the circle of Oneness. Don't be afraid to get involved with people. Involvement with others is healthy. In fact, contrary to what you might expect, recent research shows that people who have more social contacts get fewer colds.

What are the sources of support? There are the usual sources—family, friends, co-workers, and colleagues in other organizations, and professional helpers such as counselors, ministers, priests, rabbis, other clergy, and doctors. Do not ignore the support from the unexpected. When one woman lost a close friend, her greatest support came from her grandchildren, who seemed to understand her feelings better than anyone else. Another person we know, Mark, got support from a homeless person he was helping. Mark had volunteered to serve sand-

Don't be afraid to get involved with people. Involvement with others is healthy.

wiches and hot chocolate from a charity van. The night was cold and rainy and Mark was not dressed for it. But he continued to work. It was a truly memorable moment for him when one of the people he was serving said, "You must be so cold and uncomfortable. Thank you for being here on a night like this." That support was from somebody who was going to sleep on the street that night. The gratitude of the homeless person made Mark feel incredibly good about himself. He felt unity, a moment of transcendence.

There is the support that we intentionally seek and the support we get without effort. It is important to develop a support system. But it is also important to develop the sensitivity to see the support that is already around you.

Unity of Energy

The people who support you are a source of energy. Talking to them, getting help from them, and helping them are all ways of tapping into the flow of energy. In the chapter about energy, we discussed the universality of energy, its bountiful and boundary-less nature. There are no edges to energy. It has neither beginning or end, top or bottom. It just flows. In that same chapter we discussed the energy of organization and disorganization called the theory of dissipative structures. Dissipation—the dissolution of structures and their reorganization—is occurring all the time. We only become aware of it at dramatic moments. Many events probably led to the changes in the organization that resulted in Kevin being fired. He was aware of them only at that moment. And at the same time, Kevin was moving toward new work, toward consulting. But as our story ends, he is not yet aware of the reorganization of his structures.

Kevin might have played a greater role in the change in his circumstances without being consciously aware of it. At the beginning of the story, Kevin "wished he could always work from home." When our wishes are strong enough, they may set up vibratory fields that affect the energy around us. This is a spiritual approach to change that we can call *intentionality*. The practice of intentionality is the use of the mind to influence events in the world outside ourselves.

In general, the practice of intentionality flows internally from the practice of stillness and meditation described in the chapter on harmony. If you have been doing the applications in which you opened your energy centers and ended with affirmations, you have been practicing intentionality. It may sound strange, but the internal energy of your mind may be used to effect changes on external energy or matter. Edgar Mitchell (1996), a former astronaut, educated as an engineer, defined intentionality as "the active process of desiring or intending an action. Action requires the movement, or transformation, of energy—something each of us does every moment of our lives." He said that this process is "merely a means of managing energy." Mitchell points out that some people can practice

intentionality more easily than others. He believes that all people are able to do this when young, but that we often inhibit our
abilities as we grow up because the idea that we can practice
intentionality is not generally accepted. From your own experience you may know that some people are better at this than others. For example, some people can go to a dentist and decide

> *When you enter a state of harmony through the practice
> of stillness, the energy of your mind can be harnessed to
> influence success in goal setting, job seeking, work
> performance, and other aspects of career—indeed, of life.*

they will not be in pain. They will feel sensations, but not pain.
Other people require drugs to help them reduce the pain. The
common expression for this is "mind over matter."

When you enter a state of harmony through the practice of
stillness, the energy of your mind can be harnessed to influence
success in goal setting, job seeking, work performance, and other
aspects of career—indeed, of life. As you have seen previously, if
you have used or read the meditations at the end of each chapter, useful techniques include visualization, affirmation, and
concentration on the energy centers of the body. In visualization, individuals project themselves into a scene in which the
desired result is achieved. In carrying out visualizations, the
emphasis is on picturing the scene as if it were happening in the
present. The more details that can be brought to the scene—of
persons, place, objects, colors, sounds, and scents—the more
successful the practice is likely to be. In preparing your affirmations, you need to focus on the here and now. Express your affirmations in the present tense.

Intentionality can also be associated with prayer or petition.
A number of studies have shown that prayer is effective in
healing patients for whom the prayers are said. This is true
whether the patient is saying the prayer or whether it is said by
someone else, even when the patient is not aware that the prayers
are being said. The effectiveness of prayer in healing is being

investigated in research carried out in respected medical institutions including Harvard University Medical School and the National Institute for Health Care and Research. Research on the healing role of spirituality has been published in such mainstream journals as the *Journal of the American Medical Association*. At recent meetings of the American Psychological Association, a number of papers have been presented on this subject.

You may find it difficult to accept the idea that intentionality works. It certainly seems strange that we can affect external events by our minds. There are, however, relatively recent observations in physics and other so-called hard sciences that suggest answers.

The first idea is connectedness. This is the notion that everything in the universe is in some way connected to everything else. Indeed, that is the theme of this chapter—unity. Much of the belief in many religions is based on a belief in connections that cannot be seen. In day-to-day activities, people behave charitably toward one another even when they have no apparent relationship. Mark, the man who fed the homeless, is an example.

The second idea is found in chaos, or complexity, theory. Chaos theory is being used to explain previously unseen connections between events. The events may be far apart in space or time, and there is no clear line of cause and effect. Here is an example of a clear line of cause and effect. If you want to push this book off a table, you can use your hand, you can use a ten-foot pole held in your hand, or you can set up an elaborate machine that will trigger the ten-foot pole. In any case, the cause of the fall of the book can be traced back in a straight line. Chaos theory is being used to explain events that have no straight line of cause and effect.

This remote effect is also known as "non-localness." Non-localness is embedded in the very notion of the now-common expression *quantum leap*. In a quantum leap, a particle vanishes from one place and appears in another at precisely the same time. How is this possible? We haven't a clue. Nor do any of the scientists working today. They can test this with their instruments and record it with their instruments, but they cannot explain it. Writing in the *New York Times Magazine*, Timothy

Ferris (1996) described an experiment at the University of California at Berkeley. In the experiment, photons, the carriers of light, were observed quantum leaping at twice the speed of light. That is, had they actually, physically, crossed the space, they would have done so at twice the speed of light. However, photons are the carriers of light; they cannot move at two times their own speed. How did this happen? No one knows.

The explanations being offered by the community of scientists often seem as mystical as the observations they are trying to explain. Some scientists think there are hidden forces at work, forces that have yet to be discovered. Other scientists think there are parallel worlds to ours and the particles move back and forth among the worlds. Still others believe that time goes both forward (the way we ordinarily experience it) and backward. Then, since the past is still out there somewhere, the particles are able to reenter it. Any or all of these explanations of quantum phenomena may also be explanations of the power and workings of intentionality.

You may want to use intentionality to bring about changes in your career. You can use intentionality to change the work you are doing, to make your work easier, to make your work more meaningful, or even to get a job. A couple we know wanted to move to a particular part of the United States. Their children had moved there, and they were spending more and more time on airplanes visiting them. The couple thought about moving a lot. They even began to look at homes in the new area and imagined living in them. However, they still had no idea of how they could move their work to a completely different location. She was a professor and he was a department store buyer. They thought and talked about moving, but really did nothing concrete (or linear) about finding jobs. Then, stuck in the house because of bad weather, she began wandering on the Internet. She found herself looking at a set of job listings she hadn't even known was available. There in the listing was one job, in her field, in the very city they had been thinking about. What's more, the job description described her talents, her gifts precisely. She applied, was interviewed, and moved. But what about her husband? He took a chance and left his job. Once in the new city,

he too found a job opening in his field the very first day he
looked in the newspaper, and he was hired for the job within
days of applying.

In our story, Kevin has put the energy out in the universe by
"wishing" he could work at home. He can strengthen the energy
behind this through meditation with visualization and affirmations. He can visualize himself working at his home computer
with stacks of consulting contracts nearby. He can also visualize
himself in an office shaking hands with the manager who has
just offered him another lucrative contract. He can affirm his
visualizations by saying: "I work at home as a successful consultant. My consulting career is successful. I earn $10,000 from my
consulting each month."

Unity of Spirit

In the last section, we talked about the connections among
energy, intentionality, and achieving what you want in your
career and other aspects of your life. The key word in that sentence is *connections*. Connections form the experience of unity
of spirit. There are five C's of connectedness:

▪ Congruence, or being at one with yourself

▪ Companionship, or being close to your partner and friends

▪ Community, or a sense of belonging with others

▪ Culture, or having a sense of connection to your roots

▪ Communion, or having a sense of connection to the cosmos

Congruence is the sense of oneness or being at one with
yourself. It returns us to the sense of harmony. When you are
congruent you feel comfortable in your own skin. You accept
your gifts and you also accept your imperfections. You recognize
the wholeness that your gifts and imperfections create in you.
You accept that you are a unique individual and that no one else
has exactly that combination of characteristics. Because you recognize your individuality, you recognize the individuality of others. Therefore you neither envy others or lord it over them.

Finally, your actions and your thoughts are one. You do not pretend to be other than what you are. If you really enjoy being a couch potato and watching television comedies at night, you do not pretend to your friends that you are really reading historical treatises.

Companionship means living intimately with your partner and friends. Of course, this does not mean that you must live in close physical proximity. It means "being there" for the people close to you. It requires the capacity to share yourself, your thoughts, your physical energy, your activities. Companionship also requires the capacity to accept the sharing of others. It means not shying away when others offer their thoughts or gifts or invite you to participate with them. You are a companion when you invite someone to visit and give them the date and time instead of just saying, "We really ought to get together some time." Companionship is unity with others close to you.

Community is a sense of belonging with others. A community is any group of people who share common interests. The common interests that bond a community may include work, a neighborhood, religion, or anything else humans are interested in. There is a difference between a community and an aggregate of people. Your neighborhood is not a community unless there are common interests around which people gather. The interests can be the general well-being of the geographic area or the people in it. Communities are based on exchanges of information and sentiment. "Trekkies" form a community of people with strong interests in the "Star Trek" adventures. They do more than watch the television program. They exchange information at meetings, over the Internet, and by mail. Community is unity with others who have similar interests. Chapter 4 deals at length with community.

Culture is having a sense of connection to your roots. This means having an awareness and appreciation of the history, stories, art, music, and other human productions of a group of people. As you think of the culture or cultures that form your roots, one of the connections you may most easily identify is the connection to particular foods. If you think of yourself as part of the culture of the American southwest, for example, you may think of Tex-Mex as the food of home. On the other hand, if you connect to the culture of New England, you may think of clam chowder and lobster as your "native" dishes. Culture is the unity we have with the products of human work associated with a particular geographic area or group of people.

Communion is having a sense of connection to the cosmos. And this is where we began these reflections. Communion is the transcendent unity, the unity of spirit.

Unity and Spirituality—
Some Concluding Thoughts

Perhaps the Beatles said it best, "Love, love, love, all you need is love." Unity is about loving yourself, loving your work, loving others, and loving your life. As the Apostle Paul wrote in the Bible (I Corinthians, Chapter 13), "Faith, hope, and love, abide these three. But of them, the greatest of these is love." Why is love the greatest of them all? Love creates change, harmony, and balance, and is created by them.

Love is another word for abundance. Pierre Teilhard de Chardin (1969) wrote of love, "It is a sacred reserve of energy."

Unity is about loving yourself, loving your work, loving others, and loving your life.

And Gibran (1951) connected love, abundance, and work when he wrote, "Work is love made visible."

Throughout this book, that is the message we have conveyed. All aspects of your life are connected to one another. You are yourself connected to all other people. You are yourself connected to and part of the energy of the universe. The universe is one and you are a part of the one. This is true whether you are aware of it or not. We believe that your life and your work will be better—more enjoyable for you and more productive for the world—if you are conscious of the unity, and act on that consciousness.

Applications

This chapter helped us examine the meaning of unity. The next exercises are designed to help you in the following ways:

- To let go of a job and cope with the anxieties of seeking a new job

- To identify your career-support system

- To understand how the seven themes of the book come together for you

- To experience unity of spirit

Application 1: Letting Go

The purpose of this exercise is to help you see that you can let go of a job and retain your unity. People hang onto jobs for a variety of reasons other than money. One of the main reasons is that you come to identify your self with the job. To let go of the job, you need to see that your identity is transferable. You will have a self in other jobs, even in other occupations. The exercise uses the metaphor of "trying on hats" as a way of looking at yourself in other occupations. Remember that the purpose of this activity is to see that you can let go of your job and yet not lose your self. You will see that you are much your same self in other jobs, just as the photograph used in the exercise is always a picture of you, no matter which hat adorns it.

Directions: For this exercise, you will need a small photograph of yourself. A picture of just your head or face is best. Following are six boxes; the first one is empty. Place your photo in that box and consider how you look to yourself right now. You may consider your physical features. But it is best to go beyond the physical and consider all aspects of how you view yourself. Make notes about your thoughts in the first box. Now place the photo under each of the hats in the next four boxes. In each case, make notes in the box about how you look to yourself in the hat of that occupation. The last box is empty. Put your photo in that box. Now answer: What about you has remained the same regardless of the hat you were wearing? Take your time as you do this exercise. Do not rush from one box to the next.

Letting Go

I am

*place your
photo here*

 I am

*place your
photo here*

 I am

*place your
photo here*

Letting Go (continued)

I am

*place your
photo here*

I am

*place your
photo here*

I am always

*place your
photo here*

Application 2: Your Support Network

Your support network includes all the people in your life who can be helpful to you at times of stress, whether the stress comes from job loss, job change, or other areas. In developing the support network, it is important to consider all the different ways in which you know people and how these people may be of help. But it is equally important to consider how you may be of help to people. Remember that in doing the exercise, the people from whom you may seek help are not necessarily the same as the individuals you help. Also, remember that the help may be tangible, like getting you a lead on a new job, or intangible, like listening.

Directions: Following are eight boxes, four boxes in each of two columns. In each case, the box in the left-hand column is for the names of people who may be able to help you. It is about getting help. The box in the right-hand column is for people you may be able to help. It is about help you can give. In each box, list the names and how you think they may help you or you may help them.

Your Support Network

	Getting Help	Giving Help
Family		
Friends		
Co-workers		
Others		

Application 3: Seven Paths to Career Wholeness

Through the experience of reading this book, you have taken seven paths to career wholeness. The seven paths are change, balance, energy, community, calling, harmony, and unity. This exercise is designed to help you pull together all you have learned about yourself through the reading and applications. By looking at the seven paths you have taken, you can see the impact of your reading and experiences on how you look at your career, your life work.

Directions: On the next page are seven circles arranged around a larger center circle. Each outer circle represents one of the paths you have taken. In each outer circle, write the most important idea you learned about yourself. In the center circle, describe how your career or life has changed as a result of following the seven paths.

Seven Paths to Career Wholeness

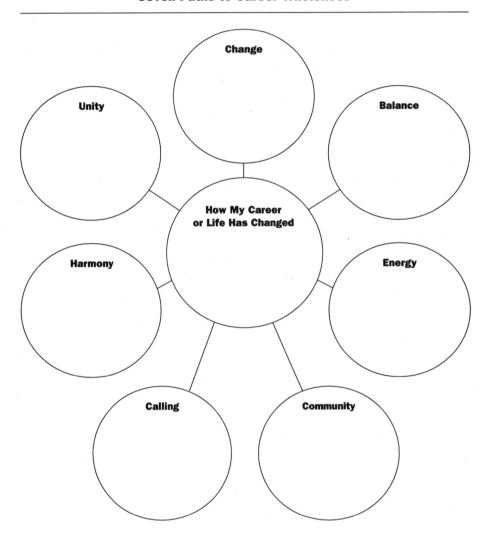

Application 4: A Meditation on Unity

Directions: You may want to ask someone else to read this slow-ly to you, or you may want to read the meditation into a tape recorder for yourself before you begin. This meditation begins like all the others with directions that will put you in a receptive frame of mind and spirit.

Sit in a comfortable chair with a firm back, or on the floor with your back straight and your legs crossed comfortably. Place your hands on your thighs, palms up and slightly open. Straighten yourself as if you were about to pay attention. Now let your shoulders drop naturally. Breathe slowly in through your nose and out through your mouth. You may make a sound with your breath as you exhale. That's fine. Just breathe in and out deeply and evenly for a few moments. Let your breath return to normal.

Begin to feel the power of the earth wherever your body is in contact with the floor or chair. Maintain your contact with the abundant power of the physical, material world. Let the energy of the brown and red earth, its dryness, its moist fertility enter your body. Keep the earth's energy within you. At the same time, become aware of the top of your head. Imagine you can feel the electricity of all the spirit in the cosmos. As you draw in one breath, draw in the abundance of the earth. Exhale. As you draw in the next breath, draw in the light of the cosmos. Picture this as you breathe in and out. Any time you lose your concentration in the exercise, just return to your breathing.

Move your attention to the first energy center, the one at the base of your spine. See the red disk spinning at that energy center. Breathe in and out of the red disk several times.

Now move your attention to your pelvis. Picture an orange disk spinning around your pelvis. This is the energy of your second energy center. Breathe into the orange disk.

Move your attention to the third energy center at your mid-section. See the yellow disk spinning at that energy center. Breathe in and out of the yellow disk.

Now focus your attention on the middle of your chest, at your heart. See the green disk of this energy center. Spin the green disk with your breath.

Focus your attention on your throat. Picture the blue disk spinning at your throat. Breathe in and out of the blue disk. Keep the blue disk spinning.

Now move your attention to the middle of your forehead. This is the energy center of your third eye. Picture a purple disk spinning at this energy center. Breathe in and out of the purple disk.

Now move your attention to the top of your head, the crown of your skull. There is a white disk that you can spin with your breath. Spin the disk. Allow the whiteness, the combination of all colors, to fill your body. Each time you breathe in, feel the whiteness move down your body. Keep spinning the white disk. Picture your crown energy center as streams of light shining out of the top of your head. These streams connect you to all that is highest, bringing all that is best in you out and all that is best in the universe in. This is the light of the cosmos, emanating from you and illuminating you. You are one with the light of the cosmos. You are one with the spirit of all things. Breathe in the spirit and enjoy the light that shines in your body.

Now gather all the disks at your feet, the red disk, the orange and yellow ones, the green, the blue, the purple, and the white. Spin them all at once by breathing in and out of the disks. As you breathe in, slide the disks up the right side of your body. As you breathe out, slide them down the left side. In, up the right side. Out, down the left side. The disks are again at your feet. This time as you breathe in, draw them up the front of your body. Exhale, and let them slide down your back. In, up your front. Out, down your back. For the last time, gather all the disks at your feet. Take a very deep breath and draw them up through your body to your crown chakra. As you exhale, let all the colors shower around your body. Enjoy the shower of unity. Let your breathing return to normal. Keep your eyes closed. Repeat the following affirmations four times:

I am at one with myself.
I am at one with the universe.
The universe and I are one.

When you are ready, slowly open your eyes.

Application 5: In Your Own Voice—
Continuing the Journal

You have been keeping a journal to help you become more aware of the messages that come to you regardless of their source. You acquired a notebook that you have used only for this journal. By recording your thoughts and the events in your life, you have opened yourself to the synchronicity of your own life.

You recorded your thoughts on the stories of Allison, Helen, Bob, Beatrice, Manny, David, and Kevin. You have reflected on books you've read, songs you've heard, or other sources. In so doing, you have recorded your thoughts and feelings about yourself, about your own life. You recorded your thoughts on change, balance, energy, community, calling, harmony, and unity. By doing this, you have recorded your ideas on the seven aspects of spirituality and their relationship to your work and life.

We urge you to continue to keep your journal, and from time to time, but no less than once a month, to reread it. Look for the connections among voices, ideas, and your evolving career.

Bibliography

Barber, R. (1961). *Arthur of Albion: An introduction to the Arthurian literature and legends of England.* Lanham, MD: Barnes & Noble Books.

Bloch, D. P. (1998a). *How to have a winning job interview* (3rd ed.). Lincolnwood, IL: VGM Career Horizons/NTC Contemporary.

Bloch, D. P. (1998b). *How to write a winning resume* (4th ed.). Lincolnwood, IL: VGM Career Horizons/NTC Contemporary.

Bosnak, R. (1996). *Tracks in the wilderness of dreaming: Exploring interior landscape through practical dreamwork.* New York: Dell.

Campbell, J., & Moyers, B. (1988). *The power of myth.* New York: Doubleday.

Canetti, E. (1984). *Crowds and power* (C. Stewart, Trans.). New York: Farrar, Straus & Giroux. (Original work published 1960)

Chatwin, B. (1987). *The songlines.* New York: Penguin Books.

Chief Seattle (1991). In E. Roberts & E. Amidon (Eds.), *Earth prayers from around the world: 365 prayers, poems and invocations for honoring the earth.* San Francisco: Harper San Francisco.

Corinthians I. The Holy Bible (new revised standard version). Oxford, New York, Toronto: Oxford University Press.

Covey, S. (1989). *Seven habits of highly effective people.* New York: Simon & Schuster.

Csikszentmihalyi, M. (1990). *Flow: The psychology of optimal experience.* New York: HarperCollins.

Donne, J. (1952). Devotions upon Emergent Occasions, Meditation 17. In C. M. Coffin (Ed.), *The complete poetry and selected prose of John Donne*. New York: Modern Library. (Original work published 1624)

Erikson, E. H. (1963). *Childhood and society* (2nd ed.). New York: Norton.

Etzioni, A. (1994). *The spirit of community: The reinvention of American society*. New York: Touchstone.

Ferris, T. (1996, September 20). Weirdness makes sense. *New York Times Magazine*, pp. 143–146.

FIRO-B™ (1996). Self-scorable booklet and answer sheet. Palo Alto, CA: Consulting Psychologists Press.

Frankl, V. E. (1967). *Psychotherapy and existentialism*. New York: Simon & Schuster.

Frankl, V. E. (1972). *The doctor and the soul*. New York: Knopf.

Frankl, V. E. (1992). *Man's search for meaning*. Boston,: Beacon Press. (Original work published 1963)

Frost, R. (1949a). For once then something. In *Complete poems of Robert Frost*. Austin, TX: Holt Rinehart and Winston.

Frost, R. (1949b). Two tramps in mud-time. In *Complete poems of Robert Frost*. Austin, TX: Holt Rinehart and Winston.

Genesis, Book of (1985). *Tanakh: The holy scriptures*. Philadelphia: Jewish Publication Society.

Gibran, K. (1951). *The prophet*. New York: Knopf.

Hall, D. (1993). *Life work*. Boston: Beacon Press

Handy, C. B. (1989). *Age of unreason*. Boston: Harvard Business School Press.

Heilbrun, C. G. (1988). *Writing a woman's life*. New York: Ballantine.

Hillel (1945). *Sayings of the fathers* (J. H. Hertz, Trans.). New York: Behrman House. (Original work published c. 1st century BCE)

Hoffer, E. (1955). *The passionate state of mind and other aphorisms*. New York: HarperCollins.

Holland, J. L. (1985). *Making vocational choices: A theory of vocational personalities and work environments* (2nd ed.). Englewood Cliffs, NJ: Prentice-Hall.

Holland, J. L., Powell, A., & Fritzsche, B. A. (1994). *The self-directed search professional user's guide*. Odessa, FL: Psychological Assessment Resources.

Hopkins, G. M. (1962). Pied beauty. In L. Untermeyer (Ed.), *Modern British poetry*. Orlando, FL: Harcourt Brace. (Original work published 1918)

James, W. (1902). *The varieties of religious experience: A study in human nature*. New York: Modern Library.

Jung, C. G. (1933). *Modern man in search of a soul* (W. S. Dell & C. F. Baynes, Trans.). Orlando, FL: Harcourt Brace. (Original work published 1931)

Jung, C. G. (1971). On synchronicity. In J. Campbell (Ed.), *The portable Jung.* New York: Penguin Books. (Original work given as a lecture in 1953)

Krishnamurti, J. (1992). *On right livelihood.* San Francisco: Harper San Francisco. (Original work published 1958)

Lao Tsu (1989). *Tao Te Ching* (G.-F Feng & J. English, Trans.). New York: Vintage Books.

Lawrence, D. H. (1977). *Studies in classic American literature.* New York: Viking Penguin. (Original work published 1924)

Lennon, J., & McCartney, P. (1967). All you need is love. [Recorded by The Beatles] On *Magical mystery tour* [record]. Hollywood, CA: Capitol/EMI.

Mallory, T. (1968). *Arthur and his knights.* Boston: Houghton Mifflin.

Maslow, A. (1968). *Toward a psychology of being* (2nd ed.). New York: Van Nostrand Reinhold.

Matthew, Gospel of. The Holy Bible (new revised standard version). Oxford, New York, Toronto: Oxford University Press.

Millay, E. St. V. (1917). *Renascence and other poems.* New York: HarperCollins.

Mitchell, E., & Williams, D. (1996). *The way of the explorer: An Apollo astronaut's journey through the material and mystical worlds.* New York: Putnam.

Myers, I. B., with Myers, P. B. (1995). *Gifts differing.* Palo Alto, CA: Davies-Black. (Original work published 1980)

Myers-Briggs Type Indicator®, Form M (1998). Palo Alto, CA: Consulting Psychologists Press.

Occupational Outlook Handbook (1998). Lincolnwood, IL: NTC Contemporary Publishing.

O'Henry [William Sydney Porter] (1905). In *Sunday World,* New York (First published as Gifts of the Magi, December 10). First reprinted in *The Four Million* (McClure, Phillips & Company, 1906) as "The Gift of the Magi."

Pirsig, R. M. (1974). *Zen and the art of motorcycle maintenance: An inquiry into values.* New York: William Morrow.

Poe, E. A. (1985). The man of the crowd. In E. A. Poe, *Selected tales.* New York: Bantam Books. (Original work published 1840)

Reisman, D. (1950). *The lonely crowd.* New Haven, CT: Yale University Press.

Rogers, C. R. (1951). *Client-centered therapy.* Boston: Houghton Mifflin.

Rogers, C. R. (1961). *On becoming a person.* Boston: Houghton Mifflin.

Rogers, C. R. (1980). The foundation of a person-centered approach. In C. Rogers, *A way of being.* Boston: Houghton Mifflin.

St. Francis Peace Prayer (1952). In J. Meyer O.F.M. (Ed.), *The words of St. Francis*. Chicago: Franciscan Herald Press.

Sarton, M. (1965). *Mrs. Stevens hears the mermaids singing*. New York: Norton.

Savickas, M. L. (1997). The spirit in career counseling. In D. Block & L. Richmond (Eds.), *Connections between spirit and work in career development*. Palo Alto, CA: Davies-Black.

Schutz, W. (1967). *Joy*. New York: Grove Atlantic.

Schutz, W. (1978). *FIRO awareness scales manual*. Palo Alto, CA: Consulting Psychologists Press.

Senge, P. (1990). *The fifth discipline: The art and practice of the learning organization*. New York: Doubleday.

Super, D. E. (1980). Life career rainbow. *Journal of Vocational Behavior, 16*, 282–298.

Teilhard de Chardin, P. (1969). *Building the earth and the psychological condition of human unification*. New York: Avon.

Tennyson, A. L. (1951). Ulysses. In D. Bush (Ed.), *The selected poetry of Tennyson*. New York: Modern Library. (Original work published 1832)

Unamo, M. (1952). Siembrate. In *Poems by Miguel de Unamo* (E. L. Turnbull, Trans.). Baltimore, MD: Johns Hopkins University Press.

Whitman, W. (1926). I hear America singing. In E. Holloway (Ed.), *Leaves of Grass*. Garden City, NY: Doubleday. (Original work published 1867)

Wuthnow, R. (1996). *Poor Richard's principle: Restoring the American dream by recovering the moral dimension of work, business, and money*. Princeton, NJ: Princeton University Press.

Yeats, W. B. (1962) The second coming. In L. Untermeyer (Ed.), *Modern British poetry*. Orlando FL: Harcourt Brace. (Original work published 1920)

Zohar, D., & Marshall, I. (1995). *The quantum society*. New York: Morrow.

How Can We Be of Further Help?

SBR CAREER CONSULTS
Connecting Spirit and Work for Individual Growth and Organizational Performance

The seven spiritual themes that support individual growth are key to organizational success because all organizations are, at the core, collections of individuals.

For your organization (corporations, government agencies, nonprofits, and educational institutions):

Embrace the opportunities of *Change*. Balance innovation and stability, organization requirements, and individual needs. Enjoy the *Energy* of diversity. Create a *Community* of high-functioning team members. Capitalize on valuable knowledge by maximizing the *Harmony* between organizational vision and the *Calling* of everyone who works there. Benefit from the *Unity* that links your organization, the people within it, and the people you serve.

We are experienced providers of training, consulting, and research design in such areas as team building, retention of valued employees, management training, diversity potential, effective uses of power, corporate and individual career management plans, career assessment, and the development of presentation skills. We draw upon a solid base of experience and theory to deliver innovative workshops based on our original, tested materials customized for your needs.

For yourself:

Harness the full power of your mind for career success through the audio tape set *Head and Heart to Career Success*. Use your intellect and logic to develop a strong resume and build job interview skills. Then infuse your written and oral presentations with the extra power of intuition and deep energy. Each set includes two tapes, a total of three hours, developed and delivered by Deborah P. Bloch. Tape one helps you present your experience through the most effective resume. Tape two helps you prepare to present yourself through interview questions and formats. Each tape has a logical, structured side and a side that draws upon your inner creativity and spirit.

Order *Head and Heart to Career Success* ($24.95 per set) by sending a check or money order to the address below.

For information about the training, consulting, or research services of SBR CAREER CONSULTS

Visit our Web site: http//www.careerconsults.com

Send us e-mail: sbr@careerconsults.com

Write to us: SBR Career Consults
1032 Irving Street, #980
San Francisco, CA 94122-2200

Call us: (415) 566-5395 (West Coast) or (410) 250-5391 (East Coast)

Be sure to visit our Web site for answers to frequently asked questions (FAQs) about connecting spirit and work in your organization and for daily affirmations to enhance your SoulWork.